W9-CAN-453

A SPECK IN THE SEA

A SPECK IN THE SEA

A STORY OF SURVIVAL AND RESCUE

JOHN ALDRIDGE AND
ANTHONY SOSINSKI

BOOKS

NEW YORK   BOSTON

Copyright © 2017, 2018 by John Aldridge and Anthony Sosinski

Hachette Book Group supports the right to free expression and the value of copyright. The purpose of copyright is to encourage writers and artists to produce the creative works that enrich our culture.

The scanning, uploading, and distribution of this book without permission is a theft of the author's intellectual property. If you would like permission to use material from the book (other than for review purposes), please contact permissions@hbgusa.com. Thank you for your support of the author's rights.

Hachette Books
Hachette Book Group
1290 Avenue of the Americas, New York, NY 10104
www.hachettebooks.com
@HachetteBooks

Printed in the United States of America

Originally published in hardcover and ebook by Weinstein Books in May 2017

First Trade Paperback Edition published in May 2018

Published by Weinstein Books, an imprint of Perseus Books, LLC, a subsidiary of Hachette Book Group, Inc.

The Hachette Speakers Bureau provides a wide range of authors for speaking events. To find out more, go to www.hachettespeakersbureau.com or call (866) 376-6591.

The publisher is not responsible for websites (or their content) that are not owned by the publisher.

Descriptions and photos in Appendix A courtesy of the United States Coast Guard.
Photos in the photo insert appear courtesy of the authors unless otherwise noted.

Print book interior design by Timm Bryson
Set in 11.5 Warnock Pro

ISBNs: 9781-60286-338-5 (paperback), 978-1-60286-329-3 (e-book)

LSC-C

10 9 8 7 6 5 4 3 2 1

To the men and women of the
United States Coast Guard
and to all the people
whose lives were touched by what happened
on July 24, 2013, and who turned their focus,
their prayers, their good will, and,
in many cases, their time and effort
to a man lost at sea.

The Ocean's your mother, your bitch and your lover
   and nobody gets to ride free
It's a roll of the dice if she'll let you survive so bow
   down, boys, to the Queen.
    —*The Tale of Johnny Load*, by The Nancy Atlas Project

You are strong and you are resilient, remember this. You will have the strength to survive the current circumstances. Know that the Universe is ready with a huge cosmic second wind and take some alone time to tap into it when you need to. It is important that you remember how resilient you are. Also how resourceful. Take a break and come back to yourself and feel your strength again before making big decisions.

      —Johnny Aldridge's horoscope for July 23,
      the night the *Anna Mary* set forth,
      as it appeared in the Oakdale, Long Island,
      neighborhood paper.

I think all of Montauk felt that we were witnessing something extraordinary that day. You are able to see the very best in people when help is needed, and the instinct of so many is to do not only everything they can, but to push beyond that to never give up. And then to have the result be a miracle. I don't even know this fellow personally, but I don't think I'll ever forget that day.

      —Catherine Ecker Flanagan, Montauk native

Contents

Acknowledgments

First thanks go to Paul Tough, author of the *New York Times Magazine* article, "A Speck in the Sea," which started the ball rolling and gave our book both its title and its impetus.

To Geoffrey Menin, our agent and lawyer, thanks for guiding us through the new-to-us world of publishing, and to Susanna Margolis, thanks for guiding us through the process of putting our story into words.

We are grateful to our friends at Hachette Books for their support and all their help throughout this process—Amanda Murray, Georgina Levitt, Cisca Schreefel, and the entire production team—and, of course, film producers Rachael Horovitz and Jason Blum.

In addition to the many Coasties who feature so prominently in the book, we are also grateful to those members of the US Coast Guard who helped in reconstructing these events three years later. We acknowledge the contributions of Jordan P. St. John, deputy chief, Office of Public Affairs;

Eric Best, officer in charge of Station Montauk in 2016 for extending the full hospitality of his facility and his staff to our researcher; Martin Betts, keeper and supplier of the complete recording of Channel 16 communications for the Aldridge SAR; Kevin Wyman, officer in charge of Station New Haven in 2016, who opened his doors to our researcher; Jeremy Will, Richard Standridge, and James "Nate" Slack, who answered endless questions about boat search patterns; and Morgan Gallapis and Bradley Nelson, "tour guides" through the New Haven command center.

We are grateful also to Suzanne Pred Bass, LCSW, for her insights into PTSD and its effects, and to Bonnie Brady for her insights into the politics of fishing regulations.

Cathy Patterson is not just a sister or near-sister to us both, nor is she just a key character in the events at the heart of this book. In more than two years of operating in her famed "business mode," she managed the many details involved in gathering information and photos, lining up interviewees, scheduling conferences, managing every detail of our project, and keeping everyone informed. In doing so, she made it possible for the rest of us to do the research, writing, thinking, reviewing, editing, worrying, and fishing that we needed to do. *A Speck in the Sea* wouldn't have happened without her.

Thanks also to all the members of both the Aldridge and Sosinski families for their help and unwavering support, and a special shout-out to Laurie Zapolski for so ably assisting Cathy—and for other things as well.

Preface

The publication of this paperback version of *A Speck in the Sea* marks five years since the incident the book narrates.

For the authors of the book, those five years have brought surprisingly little change. John Aldridge and Anthony Sosinski are still the co-captains of the *Anna Mary*, a lobster boat out of Montauk on the east end of New York's Long Island. They still fish three or four days out of every seven in waters some 50-plus miles offshore starting in about April and continuing through the last day of December every year. Mike Migliaccio, Mikey, still crews for them when he can.

Their personal "vital statistics" are virtually unchanged. Neither man has married; both remain single but attached. Alterations in their family configurations are another story. Anthony's family has expanded to include a granddaughter, Madeline Noelle—called Maddie, born to his older daughter and her husband, and a second son-in-law, courtesy of his younger daughter.

Johnny's nephew, Jake, is crowding the double digits of age and is tall for his years. John Aldridge has always claimed it was the thought of Jake that steeled his determination to stay alive against all odds when he fell off his boat in the middle of the ocean in the middle of the night in July, 2013. The photograph of the rescued Johnny, holding little Jake in his arms in front of his parents' house, still illustrates their special bond.

The parents of both men are a bit older, maybe a tad slower. But the family gatherings of Aldridges and Sosinskis have every reason to be even more joyful and raucous than they were five years previously.

Both men still live in Montauk, Johnny in his apartment just steps from the water, Anthony with his father in their quintessentially Montauk house with its quintessential Montauk garden. The co-captains are thus never far from their boat in its slip at the town dock or, in winter, on stilts at the Montauk Marine Basin. At any time, one or both of the captains can be aboard the *Anna Mary* in minutes.

Not that the five years have been free of misfortune or grief. Johnny's dog, Rocky, a stalwart companion for many years, died in 2015—still a harsh loss. And Anthony's winter home on the island of St. John in the U.S. Virgin Islands suffered serious damage from Hurricane Irma in September, 2017. It will take some time for repairs to be completed.

The most material difference to their lives, however, was the original publication in 2017 of the book you now have in your hands. Suddenly coauthors as well as co-captains, their life on land was and remains studded with readings, book signings, interviews—not to mention the traveling to get to the readings, book signings, and interviews, not to mention meeting all those people at readings, book signings, and interviews. It is, says Anthony, "a whole other job," a vocation by happenstance but one they find gratifying. Their presence at these gatherings brings to life their story, and both they and the story generate positive reactions they experience firsthand and in real time.

"It's all positive," says Anthony Sosinski, "but it brings it all back—every time."

It was brought back with particular immediacy during filming for the cover story of *CBS News Sunday Morning*, scheduled for June 11, 2017, shortly after the book was published. CBS News reporter Jim Axelrod had a surprise for the men: Bob Hovey, the U.S. Coast Guard rescue swimmer who had pulled Johnny from the water, had been flown in from his station in Louisiana to the dock in Montauk. Sosinski had never met the man. Aldridge had not seen him since the rescue, and the surprise of his appearance knocked him for a loop. This time, Aldridge and Hovey had a chance to visit person-to-person, as opposed to survivor-to-rescuer, and both Johnny and Anthony had the chance to hear what the rescue had felt like to the people who had made it happen.

"I wanted to know the inside stuff," Aldridge says. "I wanted to know what it had been like on that flight for all of them: for Bob and Ethan, the mechanic, and for the pilot and copilot as well." One thing he learned is that for all four of his rescuers, he is their brightest memory. Not just because he is now the poster boy and teaching tool for the Coast Guard's search and rescue operations, but because of what he did to stay alive till they could get to him—and because it worked. For these Coasties, who mostly find bodies when they find anyone at all, Johnny Aldridge, that speck in the sea, is a shining light.

It is mutual. Aldridge is particularly grateful for that reunion with Hovey and the reconnection with his rescuers. He stays in touch now: the connection matters, the bond is as consequential as it is unique.

In the summer of 2017, in July, the same month as the Aldridge incident in 2013, a scallop fisherman out of New Bedford, Massachusetts fell off his boat about 25 miles south of Montauk. Like John Aldridge before him, the fisherman was not wearing a life vest. Aldridge and Sosinski got the word about the fisherman via VHF radio in the evening just as they were setting out on the *Anna Mary* for a fishing trip. A familiar-sounding collection of Coast Guard assets had been deployed to search for the fisherman: two 47-foot motor life boats, two cutters, the MH-60 Jayhawk helicopter from Cape Cod, and two additional planes. Johnny and Anthony searched the eastern end of the pattern on their way to their own traps. A large volunteer fleet from New Bedford was already there. Bright spotlights pierced the darkness. Anthony remembers thinking that the water was colder than it had been when Johnny went overboard; that worried him. Johnny thought about the fisherman. He didn't have to imagine his despair; he knew it. And he knew what it was going to take for the guy to get through the night. *Not good*, he remembers thinking, and he was right: the search went on for 28 hours before it was called off; no body was ever found.

Same story, different ending: when Johnny fell off the *Anna Mary*, Anthony and the commercial fishing fleet of Montauk responded, and the U.S. Coast Guard, deploying a king's ransom of boats and planes, found him alive and relatively well 12 hours later. Families and friends had worried, wept, gathered together, prayed through 12 hours of awful distress until a happy ending raised their spirits to a stunning pitch of elation.

Anthony in those 12 hours had gone from disabling shock to riveted focus on finding and saving John Aldridge. He remembers standing on the railing of the boat holding in one hand the VHF radio microphone connecting him to the Coast Guard and to other boats, in the other the binoculars through which he stared at the sea, his body sweating from the top of his head to the bottom of his feet. But because Johnny was found alive, the recollections of that day, even as Anthony retells the story again and again in bookstores and community halls here, there, and everywhere, "do not bring negative things into my day." What happened back then "hasn't changed my life markedly," he says. "I am still fishing, still on the *Anna Mary*. Mikey and I took the boat out last night, in fact.

"The truth," he goes on, "is that it has become a positive memory."

The truth is that it was as close to a miracle as you can get.

Aldridge has never dreamt of his ordeal. Every now and then when the *Anna Mary* is heading out to their traps, a sudden glance at the waves below will unaccountably bring him back to the moment of being in the water, to the very feel of it—and to the terror. And sometimes, on land, at sea, in the car, in the apartment, anywhere and for no reason that he can identify, tripped by no trigger whatsoever, he will feel "all caught up in something," as if the world is closing in on him. His eyes will start to water as whatever it is comes closer, binds more tightly, a surge of emotion with no known source, and he'll work hard to hold back tears. But it all happens in his head, and each time, he wonders: what is that *from*?

Neither man can forget what happened. They can't get away from it and wouldn't want to if they could. Although the incident has brought more "stuff" into both their lives—all those readings and signings and interviews—they don't take the days for granted.

They try to be more cautious out on the water. Neither one of them ever works alone on the back deck at night when the other is asleep below.

Prologue

From the air, the most conspicuous natural feature on the far East End of New York's Long Island is the nine-hundred-acre circular expanse of Montauk Harbor. On a clear, bright, sunny day, the kind of day that the East End experiences most of the year, everybody's fantasies about a seaside community come dazzlingly to life in this place. The sunlight glints off the sea more radiantly than it does over fields and towns farther west toward New York City. Seagulls wheel overhead. Cloudless skies are cerulean, sand golden. Every kind of boat in the harbor—from sailboat to cruiser, motor yacht to dinghy, fishing vessel to kayak—bobs gently in its slip on the sparkling water, rising and dipping, knocking gently against the wooden dock while the breeze carries the scent of ocean salt across dunes and beaches, gardens and backyard decks.

Radiating out from the harbor's circumference is the storied hamlet of Montauk itself. "Downtown" is mostly south and west of the harbor, its shops and businesses low slung and understated. To the east, west, and south of the harbor, clusters of residential streets snake and spiral along the flat topography and fill but do not crowd the narrow available space, which extends just some four miles from north to south shore. Many of the houses, mostly of one or two stories, are sheathed in the gray shingle that is the classic Montauk look. They are ringed around and often partially hidden by thick shrubs and tall sea grasses, by stunted-looking scrub oaks and twisted black cherry trees that remain low and out of the wind, by clumps of mint and salvia and ferns, by gardens that in season sport every color and variety of perennial and annual possible in the loamy soil, not to mention the stalks of corn and vines heavy with tomatoes that exemplify summer here.

The houses, the shops, the dunes, the broad beaches, the views of the sea from decks and terraces are hallmarks of the East End, yet all revolve in one way or another around the harbor, which is central to the life of the community and to the sense of place here. So it is perhaps ironic that there is nothing natural about Montauk Harbor at all. From the moment it was carved by glaciers in the Pleistocene Epoch until the early twentieth century, this body of water was a freshwater lake, the largest in a collection of lakes, ponds, pools, rivers, and marshes that dot Long Island. It was called the Great Lake, and at a point along its northern shoreline only a minuscule distance—maybe three-tenths of a mile—separated the freshwater lake from the open ocean of Block Island Sound.

That is one reason the lake caught the attention of eccentric entrepreneur and real estate developer Carl Fischer, the man who, among other innovations, operated the first-ever car dealership in America. Fischer wanted to turn Montauk into the "Miami Beach of the North," envisioning, in what was then a sleepy settlement a hundred miles from New York City, a high-end resort for millionaires. It would be up-market and pricey and would offer elegant hotels, a casino, golf courses—every amenity and amusement a millionaire could desire. Many of the guests of the caliber Fischer sought for the resort would naturally arrive by yacht, so in 1927 he blasted a hole in the northern shoreline of the Great Lake, dredged the lake, and made it the port for the East End of the island. On a small island within his new harbor, Star Island, he built the Montauk Yacht Club and the Star Island Casino, figuring he was off to a good start.

And so he was, and so he might have continued, but the Crash of 1929 put an end to Fischer's wealth and to his fantasy of a northern match for Miami Beach, where, some years later, he died in poverty.

In a way, of course, Fischer's fantasy came true: the East End of Long Island is indeed a celebrated playground for the rich and famous, the Montauk Yacht Club thrives, and the harbor Fischer built became the main port of the East End, an important Navy station during World War II, and the current site of the US Coast Guard station. Today the "unnatural" Montauk Harbor Fischer created is New York's premier fishing port, home base for the state's largest commercial and recreational fishing fleets.

The locals who make their living off the work of these fleets constitute a unique and tightly knit community—men and women linked to fishing down the generations, or through friendship, or through being born here, or because they chose this place and this community at the easternmost edge of a jutting island above all others, and because they take pride in weathering the financial, physical, and emotional highs and lows of their livelihood together. Considering their impact on the industry, their numbers are small:

The commercial fishing fleet, the professionals who pursue for profit the wild fish and seafood we eat, consists of only some forty vessels. They go out in search of a select few species that flourish in the waters off Montauk—especially tilefish, squid, fluke, whiting, scallops, crab, and lobster.

Five boats in the fleet trap lobsters. Four of them do so within twenty miles of the shore. Only one fishes out of sight of land, farther out in the Atlantic.

That is the *Anna Mary*, a forty-four-footer built in 1983 and owned since 2003 by John J. Aldridge III and Anthony Sosinski, both residents of Montauk. The men are opposites in style, personality, and appearance. Although both are slight of build, Sosinski is fair, blond haired, and operates at a finger-snapping pace, while Aldridge, olive skinned and black haired, is deliberate in his speech and movements. But they have been professional partners almost as long as they have been friends—that is, for most of their lives. Assisted, typically, by an additional crew member, they cocaptain the boat on twice- or thrice-weekly outings, weather permitting, during a fishing season extending from April through the end of December. They head out to "their" fishing grounds—ocean real estate marked by the presence on the sea floor of their traps—and hope to haul in an abundance of lobster and crab for sale to the wholesalers who will distribute it to markets and restaurants.

On the evening of Tuesday, July 23, 2013, at the Westlake Dock at the end of Westlake Drive in the *Anna Mary*'s slip—second on the left from the road—the two men were preparing their boat for just such an outing. Evening departures are typical in their business, and on that evening, everything was business as usual . . .

Chapter 1

Overboard

July 24, 2013

"Did you go clamming today?" I ask Anthony as he arrives, which he does by jumping down from the dock onto the deck of the *Anna Mary*.

"This morning, yeah."

Anthony goes clamming and oystering almost whenever he can. He doesn't just wade and wait for what he can pick up either; he puts on fins and a mask with snorkel and goes venturing out to explore more deeply, searching for the very best specimens, the kind that fetch the best price. He has been doing this ever since we were kids.

"Did you call Bob or Marie at the Fish Farm?" he asks me now. "They good with taking our catch?"

"All good," I answer.

We're getting things ready, preparing to head out to sea for the next thirty hours or more, checking our traps and lines and other equipment, and waiting for our supplies of bait to be delivered. I see Anthony zeroing in on one of the lobster traps we've just repaired. He examines it—seems it's okay to him.

I get a whiff of cigarette smoke coming out of the wheelhouse. That would be Mike Migliaccio, our crew member for this trip, as for many, many trips over the years.

"Mikey!" I yell. "Smoke outside, will you? You're killing me with this stuff!"

Mike emerges, puffing smoke. Migliaccio is rarely without a Marlboro Red stuck between his lips. It is one reason—if only one—why he is a man of very few words.

"Hey, Mike," Anthony yells out. "You still living at Gary's place?" The playful taunting of crew members by captains is a cherished tradition aboard fishing vessels, so co-captain Anthony is taking his turn against crew member Migliaccio.

Mike spits the cigarette butt overboard. "I'm moving out of there," he declares. "That place is a mess."

We laugh—Mike does too.

L&L pulls up with our bait. They're a bait wholesaler from up-island—Bayshore, to be exact, about seventy-five miles west of us—and they're here to drop off some two thousand pounds of frozen bunker and skate in large cardboard flats. The three of us unload the bait into twenty plastic crates stacked behind the wheelhouse, then supplement it with baskets full of bycatch from other boats along the dock. In this business nothing goes to waste.

Sometime between 8:00 and 8:30 we pull out of the slip—a calm, warm summer night, with a little bit of daylight still holding on to the horizon. I'm in the wheelhouse and nose the boat up to Gosman's, the wholesaler outfit big enough to have its own dock in Montauk Harbor, for a quick stop to fill up our ice coolers—four of them, each capable of holding two hundred pounds. One cooler is for the food we will eat over the length of our trip; the other three are to chill the tuna and mahi-mahi we will troll for when we're heading from one string of lobster traps to the next. It doesn't take long to fill the coolers, and pretty soon Anthony is at the wheel, driving the *Anna Mary* through the jetty at the northern tip of the harbor, and we are steaming east along the beach to round Montauk Point.

On the bluffs above us I can see the monument to East End fishermen lost at sea as well as the Montauk lighthouse, pictured on all those postcards and posters, and I feel the ocean getting a little bit wilder. By about nine o'clock we are beyond the Point and free of thé land, headed south into the Atlantic toward our traps.

Anthony calls me into the wheelhouse to tell me about a radio report that a boat that fishes south of us just landed three thousand pounds of lobster at Gosman's. We all agree the report sounds promising. Still, we are about eight hours away from our first string of traps—anything can happen.

I am set to take the first watch, and we are looking at a long day of work once we get to our traps, so Anthony puts the *Anna Mary* on autopilot, and he and Mike both head down to their bunks to go to sleep. I am alone in the wheelhouse.

I don't mind being alone. I like it. The *Anna Mary* has done this exact trip so many times she can almost do it herself, so the work isn't hard. Besides, we had been ashore for a couple of days, and I am always glad to get back to sea. Time ashore is typically spent getting the boat ready for the next trip, which means doing routine maintenance, or changing the oil, or splicing ropes, or, mostly, repairing traps. We have eight hundred traps, and we haul four hundred–plus per trip, so something always gets broken, and repairing is practically a full-time job.

That is why it always feels good to me to get back on the water. On the water is where I've wanted to be since I was a kid. Not just because I've always wanted to be a fisherman—although I always have—but also because I like being my own boss, with no other person or people controlling my life or dictating my destiny or yakking at me to do this or that. Anthony never tells me what to do; we have been fifty-fifty partners for a long, long time. And when we're at work, sliding traps along the rail and taking our catch, it's a clockwork operation, two pairs of hands working as one. But three grown men on a forty-four-foot boat like the *Anna Mary* make for close quarters. So with Anthony and Mike asleep and snoring down in the forepeak and with nothing but warm summer air and an almost full moon for company, I am just fine being on my own in the wheelhouse. I lean back in the well-worn captain's chair—a black, fake-leather throne that has been repaired so many times it looks like it is uphol-stered in electrical tape—put my feet up on the dashboard, take a sip out of the water bottle that sits on the window sill next to the chair, and just rock as the *Anna Mary* rises and falls over light swells, the residue of a storm a few days before. The radio is silent except for the occasional hail that the two parties then quickly take to another channel. The pale moonlight and the *Anna Mary*'s lights show calm open water ahead. I am content to keep an eye on the gauges and the radar and just feel my boat chugging along at her usual six and a half knots.

There is one chore I need to do so we will be ready to get to work once we reach our traps, but it is a chore that doesn't particularly require extra brawn, so there seems no reason to wake Anthony at 11:30 as he had asked. We had recently installed a new refrigeration system, and it needs to be calibrated before we put it to use—precisely the kind of thing Anthony isn't all that comfortable with anyway. A commercial fishing boat like the *Anna Mary* is basically an oversized fish tank, and the system we use to keep our catch alive and fresh relies on chilled seawater. It is a closed-circuit system: a pump sucks seawater into the tanks that hold what we catch but then recirculates the overflow so nothing gets discharged back into the sea. And it has to be set up each time. You have to adjust all the valves so that the water flows evenly through the holding tanks, and then you have to close and cap the discharge overflows so no discharge goes overboard. You want it as close to full as possible so the water level stays at the max and there's minimal sloshing. Not a huge job, but it is one that demands a certain amount of patience and concentration to fine tune the valves, and that's not Anthony's strong suit. So I let Anthony sleep that night—I am feeling revved up anyway—and at about 2:30 or 3:00 a.m., I step out onto the deck to take care of it.

Most of the *Anna Mary* is deck. Nineteen of the boat's forty-four feet of length and pretty much all of its fourteen and a half feet of breadth are deck, and we need every inch of that space. The stern is open so we can let out string after string of traps, and the hatch doors are flush with the deck surface. I open up the center hatch—the one over the holding tanks—set each valve, and close the hatch. Then I go back into the wheelhouse to check everything again—to make sure the speed, radar, and oil pressure are just right and the compass shows the autopilot running true—and then I come back out on deck to cap the discharge. Two of our coolers, stacked one on top of the other, are sitting on top of the hatch for the tank I need to open so I can put the plastic cap over the discharge and close the system. Newly loaded with ice, the coolers are heavily planted, so I grab a long-handled box hook and drop it over the plastic handle on the bottom cooler.

I can feel how solid this load is—almost fixed to the deck. I back away the length of the hook handle, bend at the knees, and brace myself backward—more or less squatting—then pull hard. It works. The coolers jump halfway across the tank lid toward me. I step back some more, lean back farther, squat lower, and pull harder—and the handle snaps off. The coolers stop, but I keep going, still holding the hook handle, stumbling backward fast toward the rear of the deck, where there is no gate, no rope, no nothing to hold me or for me to hold.

And I am out of control. I am stumbling backward one, two—how many seconds? Just like they say—time freezes. The seconds move like molasses.

I knew as I pulled on the handle that it would be a disaster. I knew it. There was no surprise when it broke, just an endless, slow-motion recognition that I had put myself into a situation I will not get out of. I reach desperately for the back corner of the boat and try to catch it with my fingers. I miss. My fingers slide off the wood and I am airborne.

Warm. I register that as I go under. I swallow a rush of seawater, then shoot back up to the surface. I want to gulp air and scream at the same time, but neither works. I am freaking out. Red-hot adrenaline is coursing through me, and I am flailing, gagging on seawater, thrashing my arms as I reach for the receding *Anna Mary.* I am trying to run to my boat—to fly toward it—shrieking "Anthony! Anthony!," then screaming "Fuuuuuuuuuuck!" at the top of my lungs.

No way I can be heard. I scream because the scream just pours out of me, but the *Anna Mary* is steaming away, its motor drowning out any sound that might be heard by human ears, especially the ears of two guys who are dead asleep and snoring in the nose of the boat. The *Anna Mary* becomes smaller and smaller as it runs away from me, and I am still fighting to run toward it, to keep my head above the swells, but now all I can see are the lights on top of the boat. They're getting smaller too. Dimmer. This isn't happening. How can this be happening?

There is nothing to hold onto, nothing floating past me, nothing to grab, not a piece of driftwood or a piece of garbage, not a lost rope or a dead fish. Nothing. The wearable flotation device that is a safety requirement aboard every commercial fishing boat is no good if you're not wearing it. We never wear ours. I am aware that my arms and legs are thrashing around stupidly and to no purpose, that I am alone and violently beating the ocean in the middle of the night. My whole being is certain that I am going to drown. I am going to tread water uselessly until I become so exhausted I drown. *My God*, I wonder, *what will that feel like?*

This is despair—no hope—and it is overwhelming. It has taken over my body, tensed it to the max, made my stomach muscles as rigid as iron.

I'm forty-five years old. I've been frightened before. This is nothing like that. This is panic that paralyzes my lungs and makes my heart feel like it's going to come shooting out of my body. Fight or flight: you kidding? Fight the ocean? Flight to where?

The *Anna Mary* is just about out of sight heading south. I note its position in relation to the full moon and note also that the waves are breaking from the southwest. I'm not sure I consciously register this, but these are reference points. Directions. My mind automatically takes them in.

Then the *Anna Mary* is gone, and there isn't a sound of anything anywhere. You forget that you hear waves only when they ride up on the shore; in the middle of the ocean you hear nothing. The silence is deafening—scary.

I am dressed in a T-shirt, board shorts, and big, heavy fishermen's boots over cheap white athletic socks. No protection. The soles of these boots are made to grip the floor of the deck when the surface gets slick with fish slime. There is nothing to grip here. I am on my back, doing the backstroke to keep my head up above the water. My boots, down at the end of my feet, are full of water, heavy. All fishermen know that these boots are killers: waterlogged, they weigh you down; that's how you drown. First thing to do if you go overboard is to lose the boots.

I kick both boots off. They float on the surface of the water, and I grab them, one in each hand. I hold them close to my chest and rest my chin on the bottom of the boots. They are something to hold onto, something from the world I lost how long ago?—three seconds? five minutes? Doesn't matter. Right now, that world is gone. My brain is working overtime, moving with the speed of light. *They float*, it tells me. *The boots float.*

And something kicks into my brain. *Air bubble*, my brain registers. I take hold of one boot, empty it of water, creating the air bubble, then push the boot back down into the water. Whoa. It is buoyant—very buoyant. I shove it upside down under my arm. Now the other boot, another air bubble formed, under the other arm. The boots are pontoons, my own personal flotation device. Suddenly I am not dying—not right now, not this second.

It changes everything.

I breathe. My lungs stop feeling like they're balloons about to burst. My heart calms down a notch or two. So does the shaking in my legs and arms. As those thundering manifestations of terror subside, the smaller afflictions take over: my eyes feel like they're on fire from the salt; the inside of my mouth tastes of brine that I keep trying to spit out; my ears are ringing with panic. But at least I'm not flailing, I'm floating. The adrenaline is still rushing, but it's bringing something like clarity; it feels real.

I'm almost surely still going to die. Anybody who makes a living on the ocean knows that things like this don't end well. There is probably no way I can survive. No one can. How can anyone live through this—overboard in the ocean, with nothing, in the middle of the night—*and no one knows it*? The reality is overwhelming; I can't grasp it.

In the dark my mind's eye keeps seeing. I see my parents. What will the rest of their lives be like if I'm not around? My brother, my sister, aunts, uncles, cousins, my nephew. We're a big, tight Italian family. I'm the oldest child, the firstborn of the generation. If I'm gone, what will it do to the family? I can't picture their lives moving on without me. I don't want to see that. I want that picture to go away.

My nephew Jake, four years old, is the *next* generation of the family. He is the future, and one of the things I most looked forward to in the life I lived until a few seconds or minutes ago was that I would watch Jake grow up and would be part of his future. Now it doesn't look like that is going to happen, and that's unbearable. If I accept that I will not see Jake again, I might as well just sink back, just drop away, let my brain go blank and my body slip down to wherever.

But I can't accept it. I can't see Jake growing up without me. I can't see the people I love grieving for me, then living their lives without me being a part of those lives. If I can't picture never seeing Jake again, then I have to find a way to stay alive and get home. I have to create "staying alive." And to do that, I have to focus. I have to concentrate. I have to choose one or the other, either/or: I can either drift endlessly here on the waves or I can try to figure this out. "Focus!" I say out loud, talking directly to my brain. "Focus!" My mind switches on, and from the top of my head to the bottom of my feet I feel a tiny, microscopic sense of control.

What do you actually know? my brain asks me. Here is what I know: I fell off the boat sometime around 3:00 a.m. That means I'm about forty miles offshore but nowhere near my own gear—the first string of lobster traps the *Anna Mary* was heading for on her course due south from Montauk. We would not have gotten to those traps for another hour, hour and a half. But it also means I'm probably not so terribly far from my friend Pete Spong's gear. And because sunrise at this time of year is typically at about 5:30 a.m., I know daylight will break in two or two and a half hours.

Even now the sky is not pitch black. As I grip my boots and try to make out my surroundings, the moonlight lets me see my skinny white legs floating under me. So it is not totally dark, and also I am by no means alone. The storm petrels have showed up—a whole flock of them taking time from their northward migration to check out this new creature in the water, me. They are the most common seabird and no stranger to me. Small and a dull brown in color with bright white backsides, they are a common sight, seeming to walk on the water, hovering on the surface of the waves as they pick at the water with their bills and forage for plankton and tiny crustaceans. Right now they are foraging on not-tiny me, dive-bombing me and trying to peck my head. I start swatting them away, but it's a foolish effort that saps my energy and wrenches me around so that I'm gulping more water and spitting it out. I decide that the petrels are annoying but only that: a reminder of how out of my element I am compared to them. I put the reminder to the side of my mind. Storm petrels are the least of my worries. They won't really hurt me.

My bigger worries are that I am floating in the depths of the Atlantic Ocean and that I have no power to affect my environment in any way. My assets are the boot-pontoons, a three-inch Buck knife clipped to the inside of my shorts pocket, my fairly fit body, my brain. But none of these give me any power over the waves or the currents, over the winds or the weather, over time or tide. I can't do anything about anything that is happening to me or that may happen. It's an unnatural feeling.

People think fishermen are at home in the ocean. Not me. I'm at home *on* the ocean—on my boat on the ocean. The *Anna Mary* is an environment I have the power to manage. I know every inch of that vessel. I'm familiar with every gauge telling me where I am and how fast I'm moving and what the oil pressure is. And I can affect all of it. In the wheelhouse of my boat, I'm in command.

Not here. This is unknown to me, and I have never liked the unknown. The world below the ocean is not my world, and no one can command what happens here. When our rope gets caught in the propeller, Anthony is the one who goes down to cut it away—he is actually comfortable in the water. I am not. It feels unnatural that now I'm the one swimming, that I'm the one more than likely to die out here, and I don't know how I will die or how long it will take or how I will respond while it is happening. For a second I think how easy it would be to just let go and find out.

"Fuck that!" I shriek aloud to my brain. "Fuck that! Fuck *you*! Focus! Focus on daylight!" Two and a half hours at most, maybe two hours to the very first touch of dawn. By daylight Anthony and Mike will know I am gone, and a search will start. And this much I know with absolute certainty: once Anthony knows I am gone, he will do whatever it takes to find me; of that, I am 1,000 percent certain. He is my childhood friend, my business partner, my fellow fisherman, and I know he will come looking for me like I know the earth orbits the sun. It's basic. But I have to be ready when it happens. I have to stay alive so that when daylight comes I can see my way to being found.

So the goal—the first goal—is to stay alive until morning. Float. Conserve energy. Stay alive. Keep my head above the surface so I don't swallow too much water. The *Anna Mary* is still heading south, home is to the north, the waves are breaking from the southwest, so east is that way. That's where the sun will rise. The first goal is to stay alive until it does.

I hug the boots and float, bobbing on the waves. There's about a four-foot swell, the remnant of that storm that had passed through the other day—sufficiently long ago that the swells have grown lazy, turning the ocean into a rolling but unpredictable succession of rises and dips. All I can do is ride them. The ocean is huge, the sky above even bigger, and I am very small. Why the hell doesn't Anthony wake up and come and get me?

I pivot to the east to be ready when the sun breaks through.

Chapter 2

Montauk Fishermen

John Aldridge and Anthony Sosinski met when both were seven years old. One way and another, they have been fishing together ever since.

They were backyard neighbors in Oakdale, a municipality designated as a hamlet within the town of Islip on the south shore of New York's Long Island. Located in Suffolk County, the easternmost of Long Island's counties, Oakdale is about fifty miles from the greater metropolitan area of New York City but claims a population of fewer than eight thousand souls, which makes the term "hamlet" appropriate. It sits on the Great South Bay, the body of water that stretches between Long Island and the much-buffeted barrier island known as Fire Island, and its western boundary is carved by the estuary portion of the Connetquot River just before that waterway empties into the bay. Water, in short, is Oakdale's element. That, and the fact that the area is protected by the barrier island to its south and defined to its north by a state park meant to preserve the river's wildness, make Oakdale a particularly pleasant American suburb.

Once upon a time it was the playground of Gilded Age magnates with names like Vanderbilt and Bourne, yachting enthusiasts who built extravagant mansions to which they could escape on weekends, getting as far away as the conveyances of the time allowed from an increasingly teeming New York City. By 1972, however, when Brooklyn natives John and Adeline Aldridge and their three very young children sought the same escape, Oakdale had become a quintessential bedroom community for New York. The location offered John Aldridge senior an easy enough highway commute back to his job managing a car dealership in Queens, and the community was filled with similar young families similarly moving out of the city and up the ladder. In a pertinent sign of the times, the baronial mansions of the nineteenth century had become classrooms and dormitories for local schools serving the growing population of the twentieth.

The Aldridges' handsome split-level was near the end of a street that terminated in a cul-de-sac, in a subdivision so new they were just the second family to occupy the house. Three-and-a-half-year-old John Joseph Aldridge III—Johnny—was the oldest of the three Aldridge kids, followed by younger sister, Cathy, and baby brother, Anthony. The neighbors all had kids of similar ages, and Addie Aldridge remembers how, over time, a group of some twenty-five kids—and often more than that—made their street and particularly its dead-end cul-de-sac into a favorite playground.

There was a wooded area beyond the cul-de-sac, and this extended the possibilities for play. While the paved cul-de-sac served seasonally as a baseball/kickball/stickball/kick-the-can diamond, a hockey rink, a basketball court, and an arena for doing wheelies on your bike, the woods were a portal to more rough-and-tumble improvisation. The kids built their forts back there; a grown-up Cathy Aldridge, now Patterson, claims that "everyone had a fort in the woods." In winter they went sledding back in the woods, and in every weather the boys in particular rode their dirt bikes on homemade trails, constructing ramps to make the rides as hairy as possible. Addie remembers the sounds of the kids playing as reassuring background noise to her housekeeping chores, and the Aldridge home became the place where the kids would congregate.

The Sosinski family arrived in 1975, three years after the Aldridges. Like the Aldridges, they were a three-child family—an older sister, Jeanine, a younger sister, Michelle, and Anthony in the middle—and also Brooklyn natives. The two families' houses were "about 150 yards apart," as Anthony's memory measures it, so all he had to do was go through the backyard and climb over the fence to arrive at the Aldridges' back door—something he did a lot.

Maybe he did it so frequently because his own family life was a bit disheveled. Anthony says his parents, both of whom he cherishes, "were good to everybody but each other" and "were basically getting divorced my whole childhood," finally achieving the split when he was twenty-one. Whatever the reason, he spent enough time in the more structured Aldridge household to qualify as a third son. Cathy Patterson calls Anthony "a brother by another mother," with all the benefits and complications such ties entail.

Johnny and Anthony and all the other kids attended the Edward J. Bosti Elementary School, but neither there nor later, in Connetquot High School, was either of them anything other than an average student. Mostly both men remember being boys in the woods, and the shared experience connected the Aldridge and Sosinski tribes both geographically and emotionally. That meant dirt bikes and forts, yes, and later, when they were in high school, getting away from grown-ups, hanging out with the gang, sneaking some beers. "The woods was everything," Johnny says—his getaway, the place he loved to be—and his oldest friends remember him as an "outdoor guy," a guy who felt at home in the natural world, away from streets and towns.

There was a whole gang that grew from boys to men together—Danny Keough, Pat Quinn, Steve D'Amico—along with Johnny and Anthony. They were in and out of one another's houses and in and out of one another's lives. And across time and distance, for the most part, they still are. "We all hung out," Steve D'Amico remembers. "What didn't we do? We were out of the house at seven in the morning and not back till dinner. We got in trouble without trying."

But if they operated as a group, their personalities were nevertheless distinct, and no two of them were more different from one another than Johnny and Anthony. By consensus, Anthony was a maniac—"the far end," in Steve D'Amico's phrase—a crazy man always ready to do anything and everything. Pat Quinn swears this story is true:

One day when he and Anthony Aldridge, Johnny's little brother, were about eleven or twelve they decided to hide in the woods and play sniper, shooting a BB gun at a bunch of kids playing street hockey on roller skates, Anthony Sosinski among them. Sosinski in particular kept getting stung, and when he had had enough, he eyeballed the woods, caught sight of the gun barrel, and took off—straight toward them. "All of a sudden," as Quinn describes the scene, "Anthony is running on skates with a hockey stick. A madman on the loose, he chased us all the way back to the Aldridges' house, leaped over the fence, and threw a stone that shattered the glass sliding door."

Anthony's reaction was par for the course—this was a guy quick to respond to anything he considered an aspersion or insult against himself or those he cared about. From boyhood he had a finely developed sense of who he was and what he valued, a sense of self he carried into adulthood. The same can be said for his outgoing nature, as inherent now as when he was a little boy of eight or nine and his mother referred to him as "The Mayor." "He seemed to know everyone," says Hope DeMasco. "I would drive him somewhere, and he would roll down the window and start talking to everyone along the way. He knew them all, and they knew him." His sociability could have an edge: even as a kid, his mother recalls, he spoke his mind—loud and clear. "He liked to bust my chops to try to get what he wanted—but I could give it back to him."

Johnny Aldridge was different—slower paced, quiet, "never involved in anything crazy," says Pat Quinn. "He was the first guy to go home" when everyone else started "making stupid mistakes." He didn't make a fuss, just walked off quietly. But then, says Quinn, "Johnny was always the smartest . . . a very strong-minded guy."

The two boys *looked* different, and as men, they still do. Both are built slight and wiry, but that's where any physical resemblance ends. Anthony is fair with straight blond hair that hangs longish. The surfer-dude appearance is not off the mark: the man surfs, does every water sport you can think of. Johnny, by contrast, is olive skinned with thick, jet-black hair and a groomed beard that ends in the flourish of a goatee, like a Spanish grandee in a museum portrait.

The two men move at different speeds: here is sinewy, kinetic Anthony ready to jump out of his skin; there is brooding Johnny taking everything in and taking it slow. When work on the *Anna Mary* is done and the catch has been distributed, Anthony is just beginning to hustle; he'll grab his kayak if the tide is low and go clamming or oystering—and he'll pull in another hundred or two hundred bucks selling what he harvests. He doesn't do it for the money; he does it because he's not a man to sit still when there's a chance to do something. By contrast, when the *Anna Mary* is safely docked and the catch has been landed, Johnny will head for home and just soak up the quiet and the solitude.

To this day their minds still work differently—Johnny's methodical and in a straight line, Anthony's in inventive surges that sometimes surprise even him. Johnny is the orderly one, a stickler for tidiness and for keeping everything in its place. Anthony has little sympathy with schedules or with rules and procedures handed down by authorities; such things strike him as just so much regimentation. It is too simplistic to see them as free spirit versus disciplinarian, for they are complex individuals, but that they have different but complementary attributes is undeniable.

Yet disparate as their personalities have always been, right from the start, the two of them shared something central to their lives and essential to the men they became: a passion for fishing. Steve D'Amico says that Johnny clearly had been "bitten by the fishing bug," as if the passion to go fishing were an infection there was no use fighting, while where Anthony was concerned, fishing was the thing that just seemed to come naturally to him—a connection as basic as flesh.

For both, the love of fishing went way back, as if inexplicably dropped into their DNA. Though neither can claim an ancestry of professional fishermen, both their fathers loved being around the water. John Sosinski, Anthony's father, had served in the Coast Guard as a young man. Later, throughout a twenty-year career driving a tractor-trailer for Georgia Pacific, he rarely missed a weekend working a second job on fishing charters out of Montauk, acquiring knowledge he eagerly passed on to his eagerly receptive son.

Johnny Aldridge, says his father, "was always a fisherman." When his two-year-old toddler had to undergo a hernia operation, Aldridge senior recalls, "the day he came out of the hospital, Johnny wanted to go down to the dock and fish." Anthony Sosinski can brandish a photo of himself at the age of three on a fishing boat on Brooklyn's Sheepshead Bay, a nascent version of the commercial fisherman he would become. His earliest memories are of evening walks with his father down to the edge of Gravesend Bay, where they would watch the amateur fishermen casting off from the rocks for striped bass. "All Anthony ever did was fish," says his mother.

Fishing is what connected the two as boys, and fishing together is what forged their friendship and made them a standout duo among contemporaries given more to cars and motorcycles and team sports. They practiced what would become their trade early, often, and wherever they could: going after trout in the streams and lakes of the Connetquot River State Park Preserve just over the Sunrise Highway, fishing off the dock in the next-door town of Sayville for weakfish from the Great South Bay, catching blue claw crab in the canals of Oakdale, and casting off under the train trestles of the Long Island Railroad—a great way to get away from everybody and everything. They used a net to catch killifish—killies—that they could sell to the bait shop, and they went clamming and sold their catch to anyone who would buy. And what they couldn't sell, they ate. Every bit of it.

It was very likely those boyhood outings that shaped the smoothly reciprocal working relationship still so evident today. They are partners who both know every task of the job but who split the tasks between them automatically, intuitively, without discussion or the need for discussion, in a routine that has by now become ingrained. Both men have complete confidence in the routine, as they have complete confidence in one another. "It's like driving a car," says Anthony. "Both driver and passenger know the car has to turn left at the light, but the passenger doesn't have to make the turn himself to know that the job is getting done."

Just watch them together aboard the *Anna Mary*, dressed in their oilskin waterproof bibs and smocks, big blue rubber gloves on their hands, bearded Johnny with a hat on, Anthony hatless with his long blond hair whipping in the breeze. The satellite radio is blaring—anything from seventies classics to

contemporary alternative rock, depending on their mood—
and when they're hauling traps, the music tends to blare very
loud indeed. Anthony's body will be bopping to the tune as he
winches up trap after trap, while Johnny holds himself steady
against the railing, head down, a smile on his face but bent to
the work: unfurl and release the knot, open the trap, collect
the catch, move on. No chatter is needed—at least not about
the work; each man knows in his bones what the other is
doing and thinking and exactly where in the process each of
them is. They are two bodies geared to mesh smoothly with
one another, a perfect union of efficiency that the two men
have been fine-tuning since they started learning every as-
pect of the job by doing it together.

By the time he was in high school Anthony had an actual
fishing job. His father's second job, the weekend job, was for
the Viking Fleet, a sizeable operation that runs fishing trips,
whale-watching trips, ferries, and fishing charters on a fleet
of some eight boats out of Montauk. By the time Anthony
was ready to start ninth grade he was working a similar
schedule, traveling out to Montauk with his father on Friday
nights and getting back home on Sunday nights. They would
bunk with friends or friends of friends—among them, Frank
Mundus, the sport fisherman Montaukers insist was the in-
spiration for Quint, the shark hunter played by Robert Shaw
in the movie *Jaws*. As if this weren't cool enough, Anthony
even got to spend the whole summer of ninth grade living on
a houseboat in Montauk Harbor, working as a deckhand on
charter trips up to Nantucket or out to Georges Bank. He'd
come back from the weekends and from that summer to tell

Johnny all about his adventures on the water, and, says his father, "it was eating Johnny up."

Not that Johnny wasn't busy. Like Anthony, he was working after school—in his case, in a boatyard, painting the bottom of boats for a dollar a foot. He and Steve D'Amico also had a "side business" making fishing poles. They bought the fiberglass parts and the reels and line, and in their "workshop" in the Aldridge garage they threaded the poles together in patterns. Their handiwork was "kind of artistic," D'Amico recalls, and he remembers that Johnny sold some that had "tuna patterns" on them. But using the poles—not making them—was what Johnny really wanted. And when Anthony told him that another weekend job had opened up at Viking, Johnny jumped at the chance.

Now the two of them rode out to Montauk with John Sosinski on Friday nights, again bunking with friends and spending their days serving as deckhands, gofers, fishing line untanglers, clam openers, anchor pullers, gaff hook wielders who would stab and bring onboard fish too large to reel in—whatever needed to be done at the most basic level of boats and fishing. The work provided an invaluable education; Anthony calls it "the Viking College of Fishing Knowledge—all-hands learning that you can't buy."

Still, Johnny was pretty sure he was headed for construction work once he graduated from high school, while Anthony had hopes of becoming an airline pilot. He flew Cessna 172s in high school and attended pre-pilot classes in ground school in his final two years. But in the end he didn't achieve the grade point average he needed, so he quit school, and instead, as he says, "I went fishing."

He began his career on an offshore dragger called the *Donna Lee*. An offshore dragger tows a large net that scoops up everything in its path—or at least it did in the days Anthony was aboard the *Donna Lee*, the days before any rules were in effect except for size limits. The *Donna Lee* went out for trips of four days at a stretch and caught "everything," says Anthony, and he soon was put in charge, becoming, at the age of twenty-one, "the youngest captain of a boat taking men out to fish."

He also got married at the age of twenty-one and soon thereafter became the father of a daughter, Melanie. He and his wife, Liz, who had also worked at Viking, settled in Montauk, and Anthony went to work on a St. Augustine trawler, the kind of wooden shrimp boat audiences saw in *Forrest Gump*. A second daughter, Emma, was born in 1992, but another child didn't do much to strengthen a marriage that had been shaky from the start. Anthony had come to realize that nothing made him happier than being with his daughters, while his marriage was providing no joy whatsoever. In the summer of 1994 the couple formally split up, Liz and the girls moved out, and Anthony determined he would seek custody of his children. Husband and wife were due to appear in court to discuss custody arrangements, but four days before the court date, after a wrenching feud between Liz and Anthony's sister, Michelle, who had been babysitting Emma, Liz piled both baby girls into the car and drove off. The three of them simply disappeared.

Anthony had been away on a late-spring swordfishing trip and arrived home to find his family gone. He went to court anyway as planned—this time to complain that his children had been taken from him. The court, however, could provide no legal assistance: the children were with their mother; they could not, therefore, be presumed to be missing, to have wandered away, or to have been abducted. They were not "lost" in the legal sense, and neither the court nor the National Center for Lost and Exploited Children had the power, standing, or ability to do anything to help.

Thus began a traumatic odyssey, lasting for years and costing Anthony a fortune in time, anxiety, effort, and, of course, money until he was able to reestablish his daughters and himself as a family in Montauk in 1996. The first fourteen months of the odyssey were an agony of ongoing worry and fear over the children he could not find, as Anthony made frantic but futile attempts to identify anyone who might have been in contact with or even just seen his wife and children—anyone who could help him guess where they might be and whether they were all right. He appealed to relatives of his wife, but they knew nothing. He tried everything he knew how to try and came up with dead ends everywhere. Months passed without a hint. Anthony felt utterly helpless. All he could do—and he had to do it—was work: keep busy and make a living. In December 1994 he went off swordfishing again to the Caribbean and South America; he did not return until the end of January 1995. He then got work on a tile-fishing boat, one that was at least harbored in Montauk. He began his search again.

In the waning days of the summer of 1995 he hit pay dirt. By chance, the woman who ran the hot dog stand near the Montauk jetties told Anthony she had received a letter from Liz, postmarked Laguna Niguel, California. Anthony called the Laguna Niguel Chamber of Commerce and said he might be moving his family there and wanted information on the local schools: Could they send him some? His thought was that with summer winding down, Melanie, who was due to enter school in the fall, would have to be registered somewhere.

The Chamber of Commerce could and did supply Anthony with information on local schools—as well as on local malls, local art museums, local playgrounds, and every other possible local attraction—and he stashed the brochures and paperwork in his Bronco along with his toolbox, a thermos of coffee, and a cooler of food, and at seven o'clock on a hot August evening he set out heading south, with a plan to take Interstate 70 to Interstate 40 and the southern California coast. By 7:00 a.m. Monday he was, in his words, "twelve hours past DC," but by the time he reached Missouri he knew he had to stop. He gave himself a forty-five-minute nap at a Missouri truck stop just off I-70, then pressed on. Twenty-four hours after he had started, he was in Texas, and by hour forty-seven out of Montauk, he was pulling into Laguna Niguel, California.

Imagine it if you can: it wasn't just that Anthony did not know where his children were. Until at some point that spring when Liz phoned him and let him hear their voices—briefly—he literally could not be certain they were alive. There is a kind of fear that hovers always in the back of the mind that will not go away and that colors everything in life. There is nothing you won't do to get rid of such fear. Anthony drove the forty-seven hours flat out because he was a man compelled by a desperate necessity, a man in whom the need to find his children and get them home and safe was visceral, was breathing down his neck, was powering his forward motion. The guy who bristles at the very idea of being told to focus his attention on something can concentrate like a demon when it counts. It would count twenty years later too, when he was searching the ocean for his friend and partner and exhibited a similar visceral compulsion.

In Laguna Niguel Anthony found a motel and drove to the first school on the list, clutching photos of the kids. He was spotted at once. A school official approached him. "May I help you?" the man asked, adding a request for ID. "Sir," Anthony said, "I am searching for my children." He showed him the photo of Melanie. The school official took the photo and instructed Anthony to wait right there. Anthony was sure the cops were on the way, but it didn't turn out that way. The official was the school principal, and while Anthony waited, he had done a search to ensure there were no court orders against Anthony seeing the children. Satisfied there were none, he returned with the name of the school Melanie was enrolled in and the name of the principal. Anthony headed to the school the next day, waited and watched from the principal's office, and was there when Liz showed up, with Emma in the baby carriage, to collect Melanie at the end of the school day. It was the first time he had seen his children in fourteen months, and for the moment all he had was this glimpse.

But it was a step up from not knowing for sure where or how his children were, from those fourteen months that were the lowest point of his life. Now he could act. Anthony hired a local lawyer and began court proceedings for custody. He returned home to Montauk to get back to work but flew back to California regularly for court appearances over the course of the next year-plus. Anthony remembers that some of those court appearances coincided with the O. J. Simpson trial in the same building—Building 604, as he recalls it—and he remembers the crowds of reporters, photographers, and public and the brouhaha that went along with every bit of that event. He slid past it all to get to his assigned courtroom.

It wasn't pretty. Little girls at young ages were exposed to hints, at the very least, of adult misbehavior and some of the very real problems and grievances of grown-up life. Ugly accusations were exchanged, grown-ups and children had to undergo psychological evaluations, and the state of California exacted past-due child support from Anthony to compensate for the welfare benefits its citizens had doled out to his wife and children. But he prevailed. He was able to bring Melanie home with him that year, 1995, and when Emma came to live with them in Montauk full time in 1996, he became the sole parent, raising both daughters throughout their childhood.

The consequences of those years reverberate today in Anthony's life and into the adulthood of his daughters, now grown, independent, gracious women who have excelled in education and in everything else they do. But of one thing they could be sure: their father never let up his relentless efforts to get them back. His persistence may be one reason why singer-songwriter Nancy Atlas, the troubadour of the "real Montauk" and composer of "East End Run," its classic theme song, says of Anthony that he's the guy you call when

your life has suddenly fallen apart—"Because you know he'll
be there in ten minutes. He follows through."

Johnny and Anthony were not closely connected through this
period. Anthony didn't have the time, for one thing. But for
another, their lives had gone in different directions. Johnny
had tried college after high school; he spent two semesters
at Suffolk Community College and realized academe wasn't
for him. Instead, he went full time into construction, working with a lot of the guys he grew up with in the industry
that seemed the obvious and logical choice. His family was
pleased, and as a good son, Johnny perhaps deferred to their
pleasure. "Fishing is not catching fish," John Aldridge senior
liked to say; "it's *fishing* for fish." Construction, by contrast, at
least back then, promised a steady income, and with custom
homes sprouting up all across Long Island, Johnny had plenty
of opportunity for on-the-job training framing out the new
houses.

One of the houses he worked on—he and his buddies in
essence built it—was an Aldridge family outpost in Jamaica,
Vermont, on a beautiful piece of property on Cole Pond Road
that John senior and Addie bought. The guys would build the
house on weekends when they had time off from their paying
jobs, so it took a couple of years to finish, but when it was
done in the late 1980s the house became an irresistible magnet for family and friends for a decade or more. The young
people would set out after work on a Friday, drive hard, and
arrive five hours later in the middle of the night. But who
cared? This was heaven. Theirs was the last house on the

road, in the woods, a short walk away from a river, half an hour at most from the shops of Manchester and from mountains for skiing and hiking.

Johnny loved getting himself lost in the woods, testing his wilderness skills in the mountains, and challenging himself to find his way home. He'd venture out alone—cell phones and GPS were still in their early, clunky stages back then—with nothing except his wits, his sense of direction, his patience, his mind working out the path home as he went along, analyzing problems as they arose, solving them because he had to. Later he would parlay this interest into a fascination with survival stories in books and on film, an enthusiasm that—who knows?—might pay him back one day.

The wilderness weekends provided a refreshing break from the steady work of construction, for in this period—the late 1980s and early 1990s—construction workers were in demand. Even the brief recession of 1990 didn't make a dent in construction employment, and what followed was the longest-running economic expansion in the nation's history, so a carpenter like Johnny Aldridge, who had lots of friends in the contractor community, had it made.

Except that what he really wanted to do was go fishing for a living.

After a while he did just that, splitting his work life by fishing part time out of Montauk and doing carpentry part time for private contractors. He had been living in an apartment in his parents' house in Oakdale, but now he got his own apartment in Sayville. He sealed the deal in 1994 when he got a job on the offshore dragger *Wanderlust* and became a full-time fisherman—no more construction work. The *Wanderlust* trawled out of Montauk to net squid and fluke, so Johnny got an apartment in Montauk too. But he spent little enough time in either apartment. Mostly those next few years were spent "fishing, fishing, fishing," as he says, working so much that there was little chance for a social life in either community. As if crewing on the *Wanderlust* wasn't enough, he sometimes filled in for Anthony, who was working a lobster boat at the time. In between the four- or five-day trips on the dragger he might spend a fifteen-hour day hauling traps as a lobsterman. Not surprisingly, after a number of years he started to burn out.

Still, he didn't let up. By the late 1990s it was becoming tougher to make a good living in the commercial fishing industry in general and in lobster fishing in particular. To stay in business at all, let alone turn a profit, you just had to work harder. A fall-off in the lobster population had prompted the regulatory authority—the Atlantic States Marine Fisheries Commission, which sets commercial fishing policy for the fifteen Atlantic states—to tighten restrictions, toughening the limits on traps and on permissible lobster sizes and advocating a moratorium on lobster fishing permits. One of the most articulate spokesman against the proposed regulations was Al Schaffer, a legendary lobster fisherman out of Three Mile Harbor in Easthampton. So when, in 1996, Johnny got an offer to crew for Schaffer on his lobster boat, the *Leatherneck*, it seemed an offer he couldn't refuse. Even then he didn't cut back on his wider self-education in commercial fishing: he'd lobster with Al on the *Leatherneck* from spring through fall, then fish on the *Wanderlust* in the winter months.

A couple of years later Al and Johnny became partners, together purchasing another lobster boat called the *Sidewinder* and hiring as its captain a colleague with a state license, one permitting fishing within three miles of the shoreline; at the time such a license was out of reach for Johnny. Al was now full owner of the *Leatherneck*, which fished in federal offshore waters, and half owner with Johnny of the *Sidewinder*, for fishing inshore in state waters—the first three miles of ocean off a coastal state's shoreline, which are officially within the jurisdiction of that state's government. The capability to fish in both jurisdictions—both sets of water, inshore and offshore—is a smart, productive tool to have when running a fishing operation, which is probably why it is not uncommon. Any boat, as the notorious saying goes, is "a hole in the water into which you pour money," for repairs can be both costly and time consuming—a double detriment if you make your living as a commercial fisherman. With two boats, you have, first of all, a backup if one goes down, and second, if the two can ply different waters or achieve different goals, you may be able to double your income if you have the ability—and can hire the right people—to run both at once.

While Johnny and Al fished inshore for lobster, Anthony was working on another Montauk lobster boat, the *Lady K*, or, in the winter months, was clamming and oystering in the waters of Easthampton. But when, in 2001, Al Schaffer decided to sell his share in the *Sidewinder*, Johnny and Anthony saw this as the perfect opportunity to go into business together, and that's exactly what they did. Anthony left the *Lady K* and became a full partner with Johnny on the *Sidewinder*. Now the two men were both living in Montauk and working together full time. It was like a replay of childhood in Oakdale: backyard neighbors spending each day together at school.

But of course they were no longer children, and nobody was getting any younger. In 2005 Anthony's father suffered a massive stroke. John Sosinski had given up driving the big rigs by then but was working in "the yard," operating a fork-lift, when suddenly the pallets he was loading began to look to him like big yellow splotches. When a supervisor sug-gested he lie down, Sosinski's head hurt so much he was sure he needed to go to the emergency room. The next thing he knew, he was coming out of a coma ten days later at North Shore University Hospital, a celebrated Long Island teaching hospital. John spent two years in treatment and a year in a nursing home, recovering just about all his capacity except the use of his left side, which remains paralyzed. Then An-thony brought him home to his house so he could care for his father. But it was a challenging time for Anthony: the worry, the regular commute to the hospital, even the transition to life with his now-disabled father. "Johnny helped me through all that," Anthony says simply. If he needed assistance—some-one to check on his father, someone to pick up the girls after school—he knew he could call on Johnny and it would be done. No questions asked.

Around that same time, in 2003, the two men took another collective and fairly momentous action: they bought the *Anna Mary*, which is, according to Anthony, a "classic down-east lobster boat." Forty-four feet long and with a fiberglass hull, the boat was built in 1983 by the John M. Williams Company of Hall Quarry, Maine, after a design by Lyford Stanley, a quintessentially traditionalist wooden boat builder out of Deer Isle, a man who kept designing wooden boats for fiberglass construction even after he realized there was no stopping this new technology.

What makes it a classic lobster boat is that spacious aft deck, which, at nineteen feet long and fourteen feet wide, creates sufficient room for the work of lobster and crab fishing, affording plenty of floor space for big, heavy traps; for ropes; for all sorts of other gear that needs to be at the ready; and for the crew to move around among all this stuff and do the work they're there to do.

The best way to understand that work is through the gear required to do it. Think of it in two parts—the traps on the sea bottom, which is where the lobsters are, and the flotation system on the surface that marks and identifies a particular fisherman's "spot." The markers both help the fisherman locate his gear and, presumably, prevent territorial conflicts with other fishermen.

Each lobster trap the *Anna Mary* uses measures four feet long by twenty-one inches wide by thirteen inches high and weighs sixty pounds. Twenty-five of them are roped together, spaced about a hundred feet apart, in a single line—a long line, as even a quick calculation makes clear. This roped chain or string of traps is the fisherman's trawl. The rope used for the trawl is, by law, sinking rope, which means it is heavier than water and therefore less likely to become entangled with other underwater creatures. The traps themselves, even when empty, are more than sufficiently heavy to keep the trawl grounded to the ocean floor.

From each end of this groundline on the ocean floor a buoy line—also called an up-and-down line—wafts up through the water to the flotation system that marks the trawl. Just about all lobstermen mark their trawls with a combination of a polyball and a highflyer. A polyball is a brightly colored marker buoy—typically a big, bulbous, pear-shaped or round ball—that moves up and down on the ocean surface, bobbing on the waves. A highflyer is a long vertical pole, typically made of aluminum so it won't corrode easily, that is weighted at the bottom, tipped with a radar reflector, and buoyed in the middle by a float. It usually sits about thirty feet away from the polyball, but both it and the polyball attach to the same buoy line extending up from the trawl's ground line. The polyball catches the eye, as it is designed to do, because it is a bright orange or red or yellow object bobbing up and down on the surface of the water, held there by the buoy line looped onto its tapered underside. The highflyer's visibility is in its height; it can extend as much as nine feet or more above the water. If a flag marks its reflector tip, that tells you that the highflyer is on the western end of the trawl line; a highflyer on the eastern end of a trawl line will not have a flag, so if you're at the end of a trawl line that has no flag on its highflyer, you're east.

The *Anna Mary's* trawls are marked with polyballs and highflyers at both ends of the line and with a yellow flag on each trawl's western highflyer. Both polyballs and highflyers bear the vessel name and permit number. When the *Anna*

Mary arrives at one of its trawls, a crew member hooks onto the highflyer with the long-handled hook, sets the highflyer itself aside, and starts pulling up the attached buoy line and feeding it into a winching apparatus on the boat called a pot hauler. When the winching gets to the polyball, the crew member stacks the polyball in a corner next to the high-flyer, then winches again until the groundline comes up with the first trap; after that, all the line that gets winched up is groundline trawl with traps. The pot hauler raises each trap in turn just about up to the railing—on the *Anna Mary*, always the starboard railing—at which point human hands haul it the rest of the way, disconnect the trap from the pot hauler, and slide it along the railing to the next crew guy or guys, who open the trap, retrieve the mesh bait bag, and extract and distribute the catch into the appropriate receptacles: lobsters here, crabs there, lobsters and crabs that don't make the cut of what's allowable—too small or female, plus any other fish that got in there somehow—back into the sea. Then the crew members rebait the empty traps with the bunker and skate—the bunker because it exudes an oily scent that attracts fish for miles around, the skate because it lasts a long time in the trap. The baited traps are then stacked up on deck, ready to be sent back into the ocean.

A crew of three people needs about half an hour to haul up, empty, and rebait the twenty-five traps of one trawl. At that point the *Anna Mary* spins around the buoy, and the crew pays out the string of newly baited traps, shooting the line off the open stern of the boat one trap after the other every hundred feet or so to start all over again to catch lobster and

crab along the ocean floor. Then the *Anna Mary* moves on to
the next trawl, then the next, and so forth for some thirty-five
trawls in all. The trawls are about a mile apart, but the precise
distance typically depends on the condition of the bottom
and the depth of the water and what is necessary to not get
in the way of other fisherman with other kinds of gear. It's an
imperfect and imprecise method for measuring distances and
placing traps, one that shifts as conditions and circumstances
shift, but it works.

The *Anna Mary's* thirty-five trawls are in an area about
ten miles by ten miles square, and the process of hauling and
resetting half of them, or about 420 or 430 traps per trip,
typically takes about fifteen-plus hours, working nonstop,
whatever the weather and conditions, which will range from
brutally cold to beastly hot and from wildly windy to deadly
still. Underfoot on the deck while this work is proceeding is
fish slime you don't want to know about and miles upon miles
of curled and coiled rope; both can be tricky to navigate, but
that too is part of the job.

At the end of that workday the captain turns the boat
around for the eight- or nine- or ten-hour trip home to de-
liver the catch, rest briefly, then regroup, repair, and resupply
for the next trip out maybe a day or two later, weather permitting. Ideally the owners of the *Anna Mary* want to return
to a string of traps seven days after those traps have been
rebaited, and they devise a rolling schedule based on that objective. It doesn't always work out. If a storm is forecast, the
partners might decide to revisit a string of traps on Day Five
rather than take the chance of being forced by the weather

to wait till Day Nine or later. The longer the time between rebaiting, the greater the chance that the pecking order of the food chain will kick into action and the traps will have filled up with all kinds of fish, the weaker species becoming food for the stronger fish that survive—not the ideal way to haul in a catch.

The financial rewards for the work they do enable both men to live well enough without having to work for anyone else—a kind of freedom that is a reward in itself. "We're our own bosses," says Anthony, owners-operators of their own enterprise. This also means that the risk is theirs alone, as is the expense. How much they spend on equipment depends on how much they make in a season, and however much equipment they lose during a season—due to wear and tear, sliced lines, and other eventualities—is subtracted from the total. Very much on the plus side, however, they love the work they do, the business of commercial lobster fishing, and their fifty-fifty partnership as joint owners of the *Anna Mary*.

Commercial fishing is a regulated business, and like many people who earn their livelihoods in regulated businesses, both John Aldridge and Anthony Sosinski chafe under the regulations, which they find not just onerous but ill-conceived and misapplied.

The regulations derive their force from a law originally passed in 1976, then twice revised and reauthorized: the Magnuson-Stevens Fishery Conservation and Management Act, named for its two most prominent Senate sponsors, Warren G. Magnuson, Democrat of Washington, and Alaska's Ted Stevens, Republican. The Act was a response to what had become a free-for-all of probably unsustainable fishing by foreign vessels called factory trawlers, huge floating factories that pretty much vacuumed up the fish off coastal America and processed the catch right on board. US fishing interests replied to this threat by launching an American fleet of factory trawlers, which doubled down on the volume of fish being scooped up and, in the process, pretty much pushed out the smaller, local fishing operations—single individuals like Johnny and Anthony on boats the size of the *Anna Mary.* It also raised the issue worldwide that a food supply once thought inexhaustible might be confronting a tangible threat.

The Magnuson Act's response to this was multifaceted. The basic facet was jurisdictional: the Act extended US economic jurisdiction over fisheries to two hundred miles* from the baseline of the shore, typically measured as the low-water line along the coast. States would still have jurisdiction over miles zero to three off their coastlines—their inshore or in-state waters—while the feds would be responsible for the rest.

The act also established eight regional councils to develop fishery management plans for offshore fishing under the aegis of the National Maritime Fisheries Service, the NMFS, while two lead agencies, the Atlantic and Pacific States Marine Fisheries Commissions, would manage inshore or in-state fisheries.

---

* Not to be confused with territorial sovereignty, now typically twelve nautical miles from shore for virtually all coastal nations. The twelve-mile mark represents an extension from the previous prevailing line of sovereignty, the three-mile mark—effectively, the length of a cannon shot, which constituted the aquatic territory a nation could reasonably defend from the shore.

Because 99 percent of all of New York State's commercial fishing is launched from the ports of Long Island and because of the particular migratory patterns of the species these fishermen catch, Montauk fishermen like Johnny and Anthony are regulated by both the Mid-Atlantic Fishery Management Council and the New England Fishery Management Council for federal offshore fishing, while the Atlantic States Marine Fisheries Commission regulates their inshore fishing—the lobster and crab catches that are the core of how they make a living.

Each fishery management authority—three, in the case of Montauk fishermen—is required to "specify objective and measurable criteria for determining when a stock is overfished or when overfishing is occurring, and . . . establish measures for rebuilding the stock."* The law further defined what Congress meant by "overfishing, overfished, and fishing communities" and also added new national standards on "fishing vessel safety, fishing communities, and bycatch"† while revising existing standards.

Simply put, what the law set out to do was empower regulators continually to measure fish stocks and, if and when a stock was determined to be dwindling, take action to stop the diminution and allow the stock to replenish itself. Once a stock was back up to the established standard, the fishery management regulator would theoretically ease up on the brakes that had been applied earlier. At the heart of this

---

* "Sustainable Fisheries Act of 1996," NOAA Fisheries, www.fisheries .noaa.gov/sfa/laws_policies/msa/sfa.html.
† Ibid.

management issue, as the act makes clear, was the assumption that depletion of a fish stock was due to overfishing—an assumption the commercial fishing industry has been disputing ever since the act was promulgated.

Anthony Sosinski describes the Magnuson Act as "the constitution on how to harvest seafood in the United States," which may be one of the few statements about the act that does not trigger contention—often very heated—among and between fishermen, regulators, environmentalists, lawmakers, and all their relatives and friends.

Johnny Aldridge and Anthony Sosinski do not believe there should be no limits on where and what to fish for. As master practitioners of the work of fishing—men whose livelihoods and, indeed, way of life depend on healthy seas filled with healthy fish—they have a particular interest in seeing to it that the seafood they catch will be there for a long, long time to come, as vital an interest surely as the wholesalers, restaurants, consumers, and even the regulators.

What they emphatically do not believe is that fish stocks are being systematically depleted or that the official methods for measuring fish stocks show that they're being depleted.

How do you count the fish in the sea? The regulators of East Coast fishing do it by trawling a net through a particular piece of ocean. A net has holes through which fish "escape" and a bottom under which fish can slide. So how does the number of fish a net "catches" on a particular day tell you the size of a fish stock?

Fishermen are in an area day after day. They know when there are fewer fish, and they figure it means that the fish have gone somewhere else. After all, fish migrate. They chase food. They move with the seasons. They flee from cold—studies have found that a drop of even a quarter of a degree of temperature will prompt certain fish to move out of an area. The problem for fishermen like Aldridge and Sosinski is that to the regulators, fewer fish mean the area has been overfished, and overfishing means fishermen are to blame and must be restricted.

It is a stark conclusion. On a small operation like the *Anna Mary* and on the individual commercial fishermen who run such operations, the restrictions that flow from the conclusion can be devastating. Johnny was hung up for years because of limits on issuing state lobster licenses. Anthony lost the licenses he had been issued as a young man. Their operation is limited as to what and how much they can catch.

If there is anything that is depleting fish life in the waters off Long Island, say the two men, it is ocean water pollution, not commercial fishing. Both men have fished these waters for decades; they see the change. Says Sosinski, "The New York City sewage treatment plant on the Hudson River, the people all across Long Island putting stuff on their lawns to keep them green—all these things hurt water quality. You won't solve that by destroying the US commercial fishing fleet." And Johnny Aldridge adds, "The collapse of fishing inshore had to do with pesticides or Mother Nature. But pesticides have lobbyists, and Mother Nature you can't regulate. Fishermen are the only ones you can regulate, so that's what they did."

It means that individual commercial fishermen like Aldridge and Sosinski are simply being pushed out, forced to cede the business they love to large-scale fishing corporations with the resources to buy the permits and operate the increasingly strictly defined equipment.

The work is tough enough: three guys on a small boat, out for thirty hours at a stretch, working flat out for most of that time, then packing out and delivering their catch when they get back to the dock. These are self-employed guys—freelancers—which means they don't have access to unemployment insurance during the months they cannot fish or workmen's compensation if they get hurt or sick. Weather conditions and market demand regulate their work lives. Their finances are subject to the high costs of equipment and fuel, not to mention licenses and permits. Most banks don't leap at the chance to extend loans or provide mortgages to guys whose incomes tend to be irregular, unreliable, and wholly unpredictable.

There is no formal infrastructure of support behind them. Officially, nobody has their backs. In the cases of Aldridge and Sosinski, they don't even have a heritage of local fishermen families to fall back on; rather, they emerged full blown from landlocked legacies onto their forty-four-foot fishing vessel. Yes, their families would rally to them in times of need, financial or otherwise, but their real support network is the other Montauk fishermen they have come to know over the years, the fraternity and the kinship of others who go down to the sea in ships and who are in the same regulatory boat.

The brotherhood of fishermen is not a huge group nor necessarily a powerful one—although it would show its might on July 24, 2013. But it *is* a brotherhood, albeit one utterly lacking in sibling rivalry. "We're not big enough to fight one another for position," says Johnny Aldridge. "We're not in 'the game' like the big guys. We fish inside the big guys, and we fish for scraps, and each of us knows everybody else—from the Florida Keys up to Maine—and we're not fighting one another."

Maybe it's because, as Anthony adds, "most fishermen are loners." Being on your own, after all, is "the great draw of being out on the ocean." So for this fraternity of small-operation commercial fishermen—those who still exist—the ocean is their clubhouse and meeting place. "We gather out at sea," says Anthony, "maybe the same way truck drivers meet at truck stops on the highway. We know each other's boats the way they know each other's rigs. We visit each other out on the ocean."

Everybody has a nickname, the reasons for which are either lost in the mists of time or too foolish to relate. The men of the *Anna Mary*, for example, are Little Anthony and Johnny Load. Anthony got his because the nickname fits: he is slight, narrow boned, and tautly muscular. Johnny's moniker, its origin as silly as it is salacious, is one he used for a fellow workman on a construction job; the guy was a monster chick magnet. Over time the nickname got thrown back at Johnny, mostly because he used it a lot. Little Anthony and Johnny Load—that's what people call out when one or the other of them shows up at The Dock or Liar's, where Montauk's fishermen do their drinking, bars that make a statement as much as they provide food and drink.

"No Yapping Mutts! No Sensitive Drunks! No Cell Phones!" orders the management of The Dock, just a few on a long list of prohibitions. As much attitude as watering hole, The Dock is right there on the harbor, so lobstermen, dragger-men, scallopers, sport-fishing charter fleet operators, and crew can move seamlessly from boat to the bar, which is just what they do. Presided over by owner George Watson, a man of legendary and sometimes suspect crankiness, The Dock serves as a campaign headquarters for the way of life that guys like Johnny and Anthony represent, a war room for the values and behaviors and outlook they all share, and a forum for the concerns they all worry about.

Much the same can be said of Liar's Saloon, a small, low-slung tavern nearly hidden in the back of a boatyard. The bar's got a view, though: through the big windows—and in summer from the outdoor deck—you've got a scenic wide-angle vista straight out to the water where most of Liar's cus-tomers go to work. In winter, when The Dock and many other of Montauk's eating and drinking establishments are shut-tered, Liar's is still going strong. On a gray afternoon in Feb-ruary or March the same fishermen who appear in the photos that line the walls, dressed in slickers and holding their prize catches, are at the bar—or if not exactly the same guys, their descendants or current counterparts. They're as roughhewn as the wide boards of the saloon's floor and walls, and they expect you to know it.

Montauk fishermen also gather—maybe a little bit more sedately, a tad more demurely—at the annual Blessing of the Fleet, where they pray together. At least, it's a bit more se-date and demure since the respectable types got hold of the event and dressed it up a bit. But no veneer of respectability ever really smooths the sharp edges of fishermen's lives or can undo the core of toughness—real toughness, the ability to absorb external strains and pressures without fracturing—that marks those lives and bonds them to one another.

And guys like Johnny and Anthony may well be the last of their breed. "Who's going to get into this business now?" asks Johnny. "How?" He estimates that to start up as a lobster fisherman today would cost half a million dollars, 2 million dollars to begin a scallop-fishing business. How many individuals today can gather that kind of money? Can a young, inexperienced man or woman starting out—as he once did, as Anthony once did—obtain a bank loan to start a lobster-fishing business? Can he or she find backers? The barriers to entry are simply too high for an individual not born to the purple, and it's a question whether anyone born to the purple would want to work as hard as a start-up lobsterman would have to work to succeed. Lobster fishing as a toy for playboys? Just doesn't sound right.

Anthony concurs. Lobster fishing is certainly "a tough business to get into," he says. "One or two guys in our area have tried, I think. Nobody in the other coastal towns." He labors to remember the names of the "one or two guys," but he can't.

The two men manage even as they complain. They work through the regulations. They comply. The *Anna Mary* has been boarded by regulatory authorities, as all boats are boarded, but has never been found in violation of any fishing or safety regulations. They make it work—but making it work isn't easy.

There is one other thing that must be said about the work that fishermen do—actually, about the entire commercial fishing industry, the industry in which John Aldridge and Anthony Sosinski have invested so much of their financial, physical, and emotional wherewithal and to which both have long been passionately committed as a way of life. It is that according to the National Institute for Occupational Safety and Health, commercial fishing is "one of the most hazardous occupations in the United States, with a fatality rate thirty-nine times higher than the national average."* The Centers for Disease Control and Prevention, which also tracks data about industry deaths, adds that the hazard is particularly high in the waters off the northeast coast, the most dangerous fishing grounds in America—more so than the Bering Sea.†

The near misses and narrow escapes from numerous and varied hazards "never stop," says Anthony Sosinski, and the dangers are never far from any fisherman's mind. Seven months nearly to the day before Johnny Aldridge fell off the *Anna Mary*, fellow lobstermen and scallopers Wallace "Chubby" Gray and Wayne Young, on Gray's boat, the *Foxy Lady II*, were lost at sea not far from where the two normally fished off the Massachusetts coast. Chubby was twenty-six, Wayne Young fifty. Chubby had routinely brought the *Foxy Lady II* to Montauk in the summer to go sea scalloping, and

---

* "Commercial Fishing Safety," Centers for Disease Control and Prevention, www.cdc.gov/niosh/topics/fishing/default.html.

† Centers for Disease Control and Prevention, "Commercial Fishing Deaths—United States, 2000–2009," *Morbidity and Mortality Weekly Report* 59, no. 27 (July 16, 2010), 842–845, www.cdc.gov/mmwr/PDF/wk/mm5927.pdf.

the boat and crew had become part of the fishing community there.

Among the members of that community theories abounded as to what might have happened to cause the disaster, but no explanation was ever officially determined. The fishermen of Montauk—fishermen everywhere—are haunted by that. What made the loss particularly unnerving for Sosinski and Aldridge, apart from their fondness for Chubby, was that the *Foxy Lady II* was an exact match for the *Anna Mary*—designed and built in Maine by the same designer and boatbuilder in the same year, 1983, that the *Anna Mary* was built. A month after she went down, the wreckage of the *Foxy Lady II* was identified, via underwater camera, on the ocean floor. The bodies of the two men were never found.

If you're John Aldridge and Anthony Sosinski, an involuntary and inadvertent shudder may seize you fleetingly when you look at the boat that is your means of livelihood, your major financial asset, and the only solid floor between you and the deep, and you find yourself thinking of its twin gone down to the bottom of the sea and a guy you knew and liked lost forever.

Worse than a fleeting shudder, the dread of such dangers can change minds and upend traditions as much as the dangers can destroy a career, if not a life. They've even been known occasionally to turn a born-and-bred fisherman against the job he loves. Ask Cameron McLellan, a man well acquainted with Anthony, who spends his winters in the same part of the world where McLellan spends his. A sixth-generation commercial fisherman out of Maine, Cameron

McLellan has trawled for cod and haddock across the northern Atlantic, fished for pollock in the Bering Sea off Alaska, and worked in fishing grounds as far afield as Iceland and Chile. In thirty-seven years of it he saw enough of the dangers of commercial fishing to get out of the business altogether, retreating to the British Virgin Islands and the calmer life of a charter yacht captain.

McLellan lost an uncle and a nephew to accidents at sea. His brother, a cod fisherman, suffered a severe head injury from falling ice. Cameron watched as new rules and regulations that limited the size of a catch and the hours of permissible fishing forced him and his fellow fishermen to spend less on maintenance and equipment so they could still make a living at what they loved. He saw fewer fishermen and fewer boats taking more and bigger risks, going out in scary weather, fishing through perilous storms in pursuit of a more profitable purse. In a single year eighteen of Cameron McLellan's fellow fishermen—all friends and acquaintances—died from the hazards of commercial fishing. That's when McLellan traded in his cold-weather survival suit for shorts and topsiders and exchanged the dangers of commercial fishing for the rewards of providing hospitality to well-heeled tourists aboard his "luxury catamaran."

His current work environment consists of warm weather and lilting breezes all year round, as he sails the two-masted catamaran off the Hamptons in the summer and, in winter, heads south to ply the azure Caribbean around the islands of St. John, St. Thomas, and St. Barthélemy. For Captain McLellan of Heron Yacht Charters, that means coming back each evening to a home and a comfortable bed instead of days or weeks of perilous seas, galley chow, and a narrow, rolling bunk at night. It means that the height of command anxiety is deciding whether a trip should be canceled "due to unpleasant weather," thereby necessitating either a rescheduling or a refund—a far cry from incessant worry over weather, the catch, the market, the regulations.

Which is not to say that Cameron McLellan doesn't miss the commercial fishing he did for those thirty-seven years. He does miss it. He misses the danger itself, and he misses the fraternity of fishermen, a fraternity linked by equal parts camaraderie and competition. After six generations and nearly four decades of his own life, wrenching himself away from commercial fishing felt like tearing out the roots of his past.

But as Johnny and Anthony prove, you don't have to go back six generations to be in thrall to the lure of making your living as a fisherman. The lure is as inexplicable and unfathomable as it is overpowering. It is the passion both men feel for the particular freedom and adventure they can find nowhere else as powerfully as they can find it on a small boat on the ocean, trying to pry shellfish off the floor of the sea. Anthony says fishing is "always an adventure because it is always changing." The sea is never the same, conditions are never the same, the catch is never the same. The thrill is in the search itself, and Johnny Aldridge agrees, likening his profession to a treasure hunt. It is "the unknowing," Aldridge says, that stirs the equivalent of gold fever in his soul: "You never know what the hell you're going to get." And for both men there is no charge as electric as the one you get when you hit the jackpot and haul up traps full of lobsters.

Start with this passion, then add persistence, colossal effort, endless amounts of time, and all the money you have, and, if you're lucky, you too can get the job to which the Bureau of Labor Statistics has awarded the very highest index of relative risk for fatal occupational injuries. You heard right: the highest risk of death from work-related causes. The BLS gives commercial fishermen a "fatality rate" of 104.4, beating out timber cutters, who run a close second, and in fairly distant third place, airline pilots.

Most of the fatalities come from vessel disasters, but falls overboard are the second leading cause of death. Between 2000 and 2014 there were 210 fatal falls overboard among America's commercial fishermen. In the very early morning of July 24, 2013, Johnny Aldridge was on track to be one of them.

Chapter 3

A Speck in the Sea

5:14 a.m.

I am floating in the middle of the ocean in the middle of the night, and nobody in the world even knows I am missing. Nobody is looking for me. You can't get more alone than that. You can't be more lost.

I am in many ways a solitary man. For the most part I live alone. I am not married, have no kids of my own, and have no problem with solitude, even for an extended period of time. This aloneness is different. This feels cosmic; it feels like I am the last person alive on the planet. I can't be seen, I can't be heard, I can't be found. I am utterly isolated.

All I can feel is the tide rolling me this way and that. All I can hear is the blood pounding in my ears. I try to fight the terror. It's an instinct to fight the terror; I focus on it.

I know I need to conserve energy, but what is happening inside my head threatens to sap that energy. My brain feels like it will explode. I am so screwed. So totally screwed. Pictures of my parents, my family, Jake keep rushing around in my head. Am I really and truly not going to see my nephew grow up? Who will take care of my dog? What will happen to Anthony? *Give in to these thoughts*, a voice in my head warns me, *and that's how you die. Let those feelings in, and you die.*

I try to push the terror and grief away. I see each as a weakness. If I let one into my head, the weakness will spread and build, making room for a second weakness, which will spread and build, making room for a third, and then it will be all weakness. If I think about what I love—the people I love, the things I love—or if I think of the love my family feels for me, which is almost harder to think about, I will weaken and die. If I let myself feel the grief of losing what I am about to lose, it will take over, and I will die. So I can't think about those things at all. I cannot let even a single despairing thought penetrate my brain. Not one. I need to *feel* powerful. For whatever is going to happen, I have to opt for strength at every moment. That's the only way I can stay alive.

How much longer until daylight? How long has it been since I fell overboard? It's hard to tell. There is nothing here that can connect me to a sense of time—not until the first glimmer of light. I am at the mercy of the planet: I can't do anything until the earth rotates into daylight and I can see, and meanwhile the moon up there is shaping the tide I'm riding. How small am I in comparison to those forces? On land I would be a grain of sand on the wide, white beach near where I grew up on Long Island; here I am a mere speck in the sea—too small to be visible. I have a hard time wrapping my head around how truly vulnerable I am.

I'm suddenly seeing people who are gone. Dead. I see my grandfather, Anthony Antario, my mother's father—my kid brother is named for him. I can hear Grandpa calling my name—"Johnny! Johnny!"—the way he always did, from the time I was a little boy to his death when I was a grown man in my thirties, as if he just couldn't get over his happiness at seeing me. In a family in which the men did not easily express affection, he stood out.

I see my friend Pete Fagan, a Montauk fisherman dead at fifty-six from a massive heart attack. He is wearing the camouflage pants and jacket they buried him in; Pete loved nothing so much as hunting. He kind of believed in me—he was always telling me that good things would happen to me. Now look. Just look at the disaster I have become.

My grandfather and Pete: Are they trying to tell me something? Am I about to meet them? I feel my brain opening to another dimension in which Grandpa and Pete are coming toward me. Are they telling me to cross over to where they are? I feel like I can almost hear Pete, gruff as ever. "What the hell you doing here, man? You shouldn't be here."

I begin to see how easy it would be to just let myself give in, just sink to the bottom and let the lobsters have me—their final revenge. The thought is almost seductive, like a mermaid waiting to take me down. I push that thought away too—no weakness!—and I think, *I've got too many people who love me. There's no way I'm dying like this.*

My brain keeps going back over and over what happened on the *Anna Mary*—the if-onlys and I-should-have-dones that would have kept me from going overboard. I relive that split second of not-quite-hesitation when I knew that hooking the handle to move the cooler was a bad idea. I had yanked that flimsy plastic handle a thousand times before and each time had sensed that it wasn't a smart thing to do, but I had always just let the thought evaporate. The split second had been there this time again—*yanking this flimsy thing really is a dumb idea*—and I went right past it. Like when you pull out of your lane to pass a slow driver and find yourself aiming at an oncoming car. Can you make it? Will you beat the guy coming at you? Is there room to fall back? Or you're walking home one night turning the corner onto a dark and empty street and your brain forks between "forget this, go back" and "it's fine, been here a million times, what could happen?"— and in a split second you decide. My split second had come and gone, and I took the wrong fork, and now I am looking death in the face and making bargains even I don't trust with a God I'm not sure I believe in.

If only there were something to grasp. Back when we had the house in Vermont I used to go into the woods and try to get myself lost in the mountains. I would hike all over the place on my own, aware of every inch of my surroundings, never afraid. There was always something to grab and hold—a tree, a rock, something to stand on, steady earth beneath my feet. I always made my way back home. I felt then that I'd passed a test. Now all of that looks like a game for infants. I keep saying aloud that I can't believe I am in this situation, that it cannot be real. How can it be real?

In the moonlight I look down again at my white legs and my feet in their white socks. My legs go wavy with the distortions of water, and this adds to how unreal everything is. My brain goes into wide-angle mode, zooms out and up high so that it's like I am outside of my body, looking down on this little person, so completely vulnerable, with milk-white legs and silly white socks in a huge ocean with a vast sky. That little person down there is me, overwhelmed by fear and the realization that I have fucked up. I have terminally fucked up. Another surge of panic sends yet another wave of despair washing through me, and I push it away. I can't give in to that any more than I can give in to fantasies of rescue. Both can weaken me.

Wait until daylight, I keep telling myself. *Stay alive till then,* that's my mantra. I keep saying it over and over. *Live till daylight.*

The truth is that I've thought about the possibility of something like this happening. I've played this scenario—or one something like it—in my mind before. As a kind of companion piece to my survival games in Vermont or when watching survivalist stories on TV, I've thought for real about the skills you would need for basic survival on the ocean. Survival is not *just* a game, not just entertainment. All sorts of people have survived situations they shouldn't have, situations you can't imagine they survived. I remember reading *Adrift* by Steven Callahan, who stayed alive in only a life raft for seventy-six days all on his own. He managed: necessity gave birth to inventions for getting and storing fresh water, for spearing fish, for dealing with loneliness and despair. If he could get through it, it can be got through. And if that's true, why shouldn't I be someone who gets through it too?

Don't think too far ahead, I warn myself. That's another slippery slope into weakness.

But I've got nowhere to go. I'm floating in the dark. I can't see anything except my own legs, and I have no control over anything. Every few minutes I do a 360-degree spin, just to see—or smell or hear or in some way sense—what is out there, what might be near me, whether I am in danger.

Whether I am in danger—that's funny. I am in nothing but danger. I am in the ultimate danger. Now, finally, I understand the meaning of the word *overwhelmed*. I had known that *whelm* was an old seaman's term for an ocean surge. Now the surge is threatening to bury me, literally and figuratively. This is the Atlantic Ocean that is washing up against me— hard, pounding swells carrying me with them up and down, up and down. I know all about this ocean. I know how scary powerful it is, how little I can do against the energy in its waves and currents and tides. And right now I am *in* it. Only my head is above the surface. My chin is on the water, and I have to keep my head up even as it is being slammed regularly, every minute, by the swells that send water into my mouth and up my nose and into my eyes, which are still red hot and stinging from the salt. Keeping my head above the water and constantly spitting out what I can't help ingesting is a battle that doesn't let up.

My mind is going every which way right now. My thoughts are disconnected, lighting up different parts of my life. Old hang-ups push their way in—the woman who broke my heart when I was twenty, my failure to finish college. Why am I going over this stuff again? Am I really going to spend my dying moments with this bullshit? It is bullshit because it cannot possibly matter now. The only thing that matters now is to stay alive this minute, then the next minute, then the next. So what if this is my last chance to get a few things straight about my life? She broke my heart twenty-five years ago, and am I really going to think now, in what is probably the last moments of my life, about how that broken heart may have screwed up every relationship I have tried to have since? Am I really going to wonder what my life might have been like if I had finished college? What difference can any of this possibly make?

I hear myself asking my dead grandfather to get me out of this: *Help me, Grandpa! I want to be home. I want to be safe.* I don't know if I believe in an afterlife, but if there is one, my grandfather is there. Maybe he can hear me. Maybe this will work.

And then I bring myself back again. There is no one at all who can help me. There is no one else here. Only me. My body and my brain are my tools, my weapons to keep myself alive. If I let myself forget this, even for a moment, or if I indulge in fantasies about my dead grandfather coming to my rescue, that is how I die.

Think. Use your mind. The best way to push down all the weakening thoughts is to assess and analyze my situation and, by a process of elimination, come up with some way to get out of it. So I need to go over my situation again, think it through one more time, figure out what it's telling me. I know where I am: the *Anna Mary* was heading due south on a course just west of 180 degrees. When I went overboard at what I figure was about 3:00 a.m., she had just reached the forty-fathom curve, which is where the Atlantic water starts to turn warmer because you're getting closer to the Gulf Stream. At that point she would have been about an hour and a half away from our traps—about fifteen miles. So I am some forty miles from Montauk, which is to the north. I know the direction the wind is blowing. When the sun comes up, I will know the time—about 5:30 a.m.—and I will also know the direction of due east.

I know too that with sunup, people will start searching for me, if they haven't started already. The problem is that I am the proverbial needle in a haystack, and I am virtually invisible. My hair is black, my T-shirt is pale blue—colors that will simply disappear in the waves. I have to make myself visible, and that means I will need to find a buoy, something brightly colored that someone on a boat or in a plane can see. Out here that means a lobsterman's string of traps, and the lobsterman whose string of traps I am not too far from, once again, is Pete Spong. So when daylight comes I will start looking for Pete's gear. Keep saying that. Saying it over and over makes it seem real, makes it seem possible.

Sunup must be close now, which also means fish are starting to feed. I'm not sure what this will mean for me until I see in the moonlight two dorsal fins jutting above the surface of the ocean. These are the fins of sharks. They are the fins of sharks that are moving swiftly and gracefully toward me and are suddenly tracing circles around me. They are assessing me as a food option.

Another red-hot burst of adrenaline-laced terror runs through me, tensing my body rigid, and out loud I order myself to chill out. In the depths I can see the shadows of the two sharks, illumined by the moonlight. In this part of the ocean at this time of year they must be blue sharks. They look to be somewhere between six to eight feet long. I know about this species of shark. I know they like to feed on squid but will eat any fish as well as sea birds. They are not known man-eaters, but if they are hungry and there is nothing better around, they will attack and eat humans. Of course. Any animal will do so. Humans have also done so throughout history.

I reach into the pocket of my shorts and unclip the three-inch Buck folding knife I always carry, very careful as I open it to not graze my skin with its sharp edge. Last thing I want is even a drop of blood in the water.

Blood. I bet these animals can sense the blood pounding inside my body, so now I have a new mantra, and I start reciting it to my heart: *Slow down*, I tell my heart. *Be calm.*

I think about stabbing the sharks if they come at me. But as soon as I have that thought, I know how foolish it is. A three-inch knife against the jaws and teeth of even one shark? Ridiculous. Futile. The sharks keep circling—ten minutes, twenty minutes, half an hour. *Control your breathing*, I order myself. *Slow your heart rate.* It takes effort, but I feel my heart pumping more regularly. And in this calmer state I say to myself that if the sharks come, they come. When they get here, I'll fight them. But right now I need to stop freaking out about the sharks and start putting my mind to what will happen when daylight comes. I have to concentrate on catching the light the moment it breaks so I can see what I have to do next. Time is not on my side. Time is another killer. Still clutching the knife, I swim away from the sharks, and soon enough they head off in the opposite direction.

I'm still floating, still alone, still lost when the light very suddenly breaks through. They call this the golden hour, when the sun is so near the horizon that its light travels through thick atmosphere and comes at us indirectly, redder and softer than it will later in the day. Now I can see a little, and soon I will be able to see more, and this utterly transforms my situation. Like being a little kid: take away the dark, and everything seems better.

Now I just have to find a buoy.

Chapter 4

"He's Not Here"

6:22 a.m.

When Johnny and Anthony first bought the *Anna Mary* they spent a year almost literally reconstructing it from top to bottom. Originally built as a day-trip boat, the vessel had no storage below decks and no beds, and the two set about customizing it for offshore lobster fishing. They framed out a new deck, new tanks, and a new wheelhouse, and they replaced the old hydraulic and plumbing systems. They raised the height of the ceiling below decks and crammed two bunks right in the nose of the boat, plus a galley big enough to hold a hot plate and a storage locker for their miles of rope, survival gear, spare parts, and other pieces of equipment. They tightened up the hull, filled in the seams, made the boat seaworthy for forty or fifty miles offshore—or more. In essence they had bought a hull and a permit, both of which were highly valuable, and had built a new boat around those two precious commodities.

But they hadn't built a head—the nautical term for a toilet—providing themselves instead with a five-gallon plastic bucket that sits on the deck until needed and gets emptied over the side after use. On the morning of July 24, 2013, that head was the intended destination of deckhand Mike Migliaccio. Somewhere between 5:30 and 6:00 a.m. Mike hauled himself out of his bunk in the forepeak and made his way up the narrow stairway to the wheelhouse and out onto the deck. Still groggy with sleep, Mike only vaguely registered that Johnny wasn't in the wheelhouse—was not seated or sprawled in the captain's chair nor curled up on the bench behind the chair, which is where he sometimes caught a nap. Mike isn't sure if he consciously thought to himself that Johnny must therefore be out on deck, but he is quite clear that when he had been on deck for a minute—maybe less—he realized that Johnny was *not* on the deck. Mike looked up: Johnny was not up in the mast either.

This was all wrong. "Johnny is the guy who watches out for everybody else," says Migliaccio, an ex-Marine, Vietnam vet, a guy who by his own admission is incapable of punching a time clock. "I couldn't understand why he wasn't there." Normally Johnny would wake Mike before sunup and give him the wheel for a couple of hours to take the *Anna Mary* its final miles to its trawls. Suddenly Mike was sharply aware that it was after sunrise and *there was nobody driving the boat.* That was unbelievable, and it was frightening.

"Anthony!" Mike yelled at the top of his lungs and raced down to the hold to rouse him.

Anthony came up out of a deep sleep to see Mike's terrified face, his mouth moving, saying something about Johnny.

"Johnny?" Anthony asked. "Where is he?"

"He's not here," Mike answered. Then he said it again: "He's not here."

Anthony was bolt upright now, and the two of them searched again, as if Johnny not being there had been a mirage or a joke or a false alarm or a bizarre game of hide-and-seek. They called his name and they looked for him, increasingly frantic as they searched. Johnny was not in the wheelhouse. He was not on deck. They noticed that the hatch was off the starboard lobster tank. Did he fall in? Hit his head and drown? They looked. Nothing.

The *Anna Mary* is not a big boat. If you're not in the bunk-room, and you're not in the wheelhouse, and you're not on deck, you're gone.

Terror flooded into Anthony's body and weighed him down. For a moment he felt paralyzed. Memories of faces, names, voices ricocheted around the inside of his brain. One powerful memory was of the hushed talk of adults when he was a young boy about the *Windblown*, a tilefish boat that broke up off Block Island and went down with all hands. The muffled conversations—*don't let the kids hear this!*—went on for years, it seemed to him. The fishermen lost were young men, and their mothers continued to live in Montauk all the time he was growing up. He remembers as a boy staring at them with a kind of frightened awe when they were pointed out to him.

Other losses were closer in time and distance. He remembered the *New Age*, a trawler, and the crew member who got hit by a net and slipped overboard—dead from the hit itself, most likely, then lost in the ocean. There was Scott Gates, who went overboard on a wave and was never found. Indian John who was out swordfishing and fell overboard—never found. Dick Vigilent, his swordfish boat literally run over by another boat in the Gulf of Mexico, attacked and killed by sharks while his crew looked on helplessly, unable to avoid hearing the screams as Dick's body was ripped apart. *I'm always one minute away from death*, he thought. *But not Johnny. It is not going to be like that with Johnny.* Then: *I've got to take stock*, he told himself. He noticed he was sweating.

"Where are we? I have to write it down. We have to turn around."

He did both, jotting down his compass coordinates in his logbook and reversing the *Anna Mary's* direction back along the same compass course that had brought it here—north now, due north back the way they had come. Then he clicked on the radio.

Channel 16 VHF is the very high-frequency channel used for maritime and shipping purposes and for international distress calls. Anthony's call was logged in at 6:22 that morning. His voice is thick, trembling. He sounds catatonic.

"US Coast Guard, US Coast Guard. *Anna Mary* standing by Channel 16. Over."

"*Anna Mary*, this is Coast Guard on 16. Go ahead."

That was Sean Davis, an operations specialist on duty that morning in the command center for Sector Long Island Sound, housed on the second floor of a long, low, red-brick building at the Coast Guard station in New Haven,

Connecticut, on the eastern side of New Haven harbor. A team of four watchstanders is on duty around the clock in twelve-hour shifts at every sector command center, and Davis's team had just relieved the night shift and were starting their day. In fact, Davis had just put together his breakfast of oatmeal, a hard-boiled egg, and a cup of coffee and had brought it all back to his seat in the communications suite. He sat down and waited to hear from the mariner calling in, the captain of a vessel called the *Anna Mary*.

But the captain—Anthony—was hesitant. He could not find the words, didn't know how to string together what had happened. "*Anna Mary*. I just woke up," he told Davis, who took his first sip of hot coffee. Anthony paused, uncertain how to put it. "I lost a crew member overboard." Davis locked the coffee in his mouth and stood up. Another blank space from Anthony. "Uhhhh, I'm missing my crew member, John Aldridge." He paused again. Stumbled, sighed. "I don't know what to say. I'm in shock."

Sean Davis felt a knot in his gut, swallowed, and took a deep breath. "Roger, Captain," Davis responded calmly to Anthony. "What's your position right now?"

Breakfast was over. Davis and everyone else in the command center went to work.

The US Coast Guard traces its history back to the US Lighthouse Service, established by the first Congress in 1789 and placed within the purview of the US Treasury Department. A year later the secretary of the department, none other than Alexander Hamilton, received authorization to create a maritime service of ten cutters to enforce customs laws. Over the next century and more, new powers were carved out for this maritime agency—vessel inspection and life saving among them. New agencies were formed to execute these powers, and the agencies were shifted from one cabinet department to another while their assignments were variously merged, augmented, or split off.

In 1915 President Woodrow Wilson signed the bill officially ordering the creation of the Coast Guard and designating it "a military service and a branch of the armed forces at all times," but the revisions to the service's assigned missions and the shifts of its management from one cabinet department to another continued through World War II and beyond. In fact, as recently as 2003 the Coast Guard was transferred to the Department of Homeland Security, and its list of eleven missions was fixed in law.

The service's official creation may also have triggered the now-standard nickname for members of the Coast Guard—"Coasties"—and search-and-rescue, SAR, constitutes one of the oldest of the missions Coasties carry out. The Coast Guard's authority for this mission is formalized in what is called Emergency Support Function #9 of the Federal Response System, and its aim, as the Coast Guard describes the mission, is, in the face of a natural or manmade disaster to "prevent loss of life in every situation where our actions and performance could possibly be brought to bear." That covers a lot of territory, for the Coast Guard is responsible for the nation's Atlantic and Pacific coastlines, including Alaska and Hawaii, for its Great Lakes and major rivers, and for the islands of its eastern and western territories and possessions.* To organize this broad responsibility, the service is organized into nine districts, numbered as they were long ago rather than sequentially, with the Atlantic Area comprising five districts and the Pacific Area four. District 1 covers the waters from the top of Maine to a chunk of northern New Jersey and, like all districts, is divided into sector commands. From an organizational standpoint John Aldridge fell overboard in Sector Long Island Sound of District 1 of the Coast Guard's scope of responsibility, an area of ocean extending from Shelter Island to Block Island, Gardiners Bay, and Block Island Sound, plus the fifty nautical miles south of Montauk Point and west along the south shore of Long Island.

To execute the search-and-rescue mission—in fact, all its missions—the Coast Guard operates a fleet of assets that includes cutters, defined as vessels sixty-five feet long or bigger that can accommodate a live-in crew and can go pretty much anywhere; boats, which are the smaller vessels that operate near shore and on inland waterways; and both fixed-wing and rotary aircraft. The cutters, they say, are the heart of the service; the boats are the soul of the service; and surely where search and rescue are concerned, the aircraft are the eyes of the service.

---

* The USCG also maintains three foreign commands, one each in Japan and the Netherlands for inspection of ships that may operate in the U.S., and a third in Bahrain providing support to combat-ready Coast Guard troops who may be deployed to deal with national security concerns.

But the boats and planes have to start looking somewhere, and for that, the Coast Guard's prized tool is SAROPS, the Search and Rescue Optimal Planning System. SAROPS is a Monte Carlo–based software system—that is, it relies on repeated random samplings to generate probabilities. The system shows graphically how, where, and in what direction a lost object—a vessel or, as in this case, a person—will most probably be drifting on the surface of the water, and it "corrects" the graphic over time to show how changing conditions affect the drift. Data inputs about winds, currents, swells, water temperature, visibility, plus anything known about the lost object—an individual's height, weight, clothing, physical fitness—simulate the drift as thousands of multicolored particles on the screen; the denser the gathering of particles, the more probable it is that that is a place to search. As the data change over time and as more and more kinds of information are relayed into the system from the actual scene of the search, SAROPS corrects the picture on the screen so searchers can adjust the pattern of their search, if needed, or modify the search area.

The watchstander team that had just come on duty in the New Haven command center the morning of July 24, 2013, like all watchstander teams throughout the service, comprised four individuals representing distinct areas of functional expertise: a situation unit controller, an operations unit controller, a communications unit controller—that was Sean Davis—and the command duty officer in overall charge of the watch. In fact, on that day there was a fifth watchstander present. Operations Specialist Jason Rodocker had just been reassigned from Baltimore. This was only his second day in New Haven, and he was still figuring out who was who in the command center and where the coffee machine was. He was, in the parlance of the service, "breaking in" and had not yet been assigned a function or given a role. That would change and change fast.

The command center is a large room, windowless, and guarded by stringent security measures. The lighting is typically kept dim so the images on the monitors show up better, and there are a lot of monitors in the command center. On the wall half a dozen television monitors are tuned to various weather and news stations, while the two long, curved banks of desks hold maybe a dozen computer monitors each. In other words, everything and everybody in this large, open-space pen is geared toward the windowless wall and all the monitors.

Back behind this space is the glass-walled communications suite, bristling with microphones, radios, and more monitors, and that is where Sean Davis, having set down his coffee, was taking in information and spewing it back out to the rest of the watch floor with the speed and agility of a simultaneous translator at the United Nations.

The operations controller for the watch had already alerted the Coast Guard station in Montauk to activate a search and rescue unit—SRU—and get it underway. The situation unit controller had identified two cutters in or near the area, the *Sailfish* steaming up from New York and the *Tiger Shark* from the New England area, which could be deployed to join the search. Commander Jonathan Theel, the search mission coordinator for the sector, still in his car on the way to the station but in touch with the command center via his cell phone, had briefed the district headquarters in Boston and requested a helicopter to aid in the search.

For Sean Davis, the issue was the multitude of voices to be juggled, but the one that was of pressing concern right now was the voice of Anthony Sosinski in his left ear. *Think about what you're going to say to him*, Davis told himself as he heard the fear in Sosinski's voice, *and say what you have to say as calmly as possible. Remember: you're not in distress. The guy in the water is in distress, and the guy on the radio is scared. The calmer you are, the more he'll understand you're in control of the situation and can help.*

Davis had asked for position coordinates, and Anthony had replied twice because his first reply had been stepped on by other voices cutting in on the frequency. "Roger, Captain," Davis said now to Anthony, calmly and in a voice that he hoped sounded businesslike and in control. "How many crew are on board with you?"

Anthony answered with a narrative—how he took the boat out of the harbor, then passed the wheel to John while he and Mike "lay down." How Johnny was supposed to wake him at 11:30 to take the next watch and how, instead, Johnny "fell over somewhere." Then he added, "I'm freaking out."

Sean Davis in person is as calming a presence as his voice would lead you to believe. Well-defined eyebrows and a firm mouth add an air of gravitas to his looks, but the overall impression is both stalwart and sympathetic. Yet as Davis listened to the tale Anthony told and to the terror in his voice, he felt the goosebumps rise across his body. He could not yet determine the magnitude of the situation coming at him, but he knew that situation was not going to be easy. When he heard Anthony say, "I have no clue whatsoever of where he fell overboard or how many hours ago he fell overboard," Davis knew—everyone within hearing in the command center knew—that they were going to have to conduct an extensive search over a huge area. "From the moment the initial report came in," Davis says, "everything was in the works"—meaning that all the assets of the US Coast Guard were poised to look for this man—and although no one was willing to say as much, with very minimal chance of a happy ending.

Davis pressed Sosinski for details: *What are John's height and weight? What time did he relieve you? Where is the* Anna Mary *now?*

Headed back north, said Anthony, adding, "I'm beside myself. I don't know what to do."

At 6:30 a.m., eight minutes after the first report that Johnny was missing, Davis issued the universal maritime alert for urgent attention. "Pan pan, pan pan, pan pan."* All stations: "United States Coast Guard Sector Long Island Sound, United States Coast Guard Sector Long Island Sound. At zero-six twenty-two local time, the Coast Guard received a report of a person in the water south of Montauk Point, New York. All vessels in the vicinity are requested to keep a sharp lookout, assist if possible, and report all sightings to United States Coast Guard. This is United States Coast Guard Sector Long Island Sound—out."

---

* Like "mayday," a corruption of *M'aidez!*, the pan pan signal derives from French: *panne* is a breakdown or failure.

Anthony asked for advice: "What should I do?" he wanted to know. Mike was up on the roof of the boat, holding on to the mast and staring at the water, searching. Davis concurred that that was a good idea and asked Anthony to keep him apprised of the weather and visibility. "Can you send an aircraft?" Anthony pleaded. Davis assured him he was "working on that."

At the Coast Guard station in Montauk Senior Chief Boatswain's Mate Jason Walter, in charge of the station, got the word from the sector command center in New Haven and ordered the first boat to get going. It was a forty-seven-foot motor life boat, the search-and-rescue and lifesaving workhorse of the service—self-righting, built to withstand hurricane force winds and heavy seas, capable of a speed of more than twenty-five knots and of ranging as far as two hundred miles offshore. *CG47279*, to give the Montauk 47 its official name, fully supplied and crewed and under the command of Boatswain's Mate Josh Garsik, launched out of the station at 6:35 a.m. with the mission to find and save PIW—person in water—Johnny Aldridge, following the north-to-south course the *Anna Mary* had taken the previous night. Just about an hour later Walter himself and a crew of three others were headed out on a small response boat, one of the two other boats available at the station. A twenty-year veteran of the service and, in appearance, a military officer out of Central Casting—tall, with shoulders broad enough to carry full responsibility and with a winning smile when needed—Jason Walter was more than prepared to serve as on-scene SRU commander when the search area was reached. The third boat, another forty-seven-foot motor life boat, was in reserve, and a crew was readied, all primed to go out again later in the day, if needed, when the first 47 had reached its maximum allowable hours for fuel, supplies, and crew sustainability.

Three boats constituted an anomaly for Montauk Station because it has only enough staff to man one of its three boats at any one time. But July 24 was a Wednesday, and Wednesday is switch-out day—officially, duty relief day—when the two duty sections, called Port and Starboard, each consisting of some ten people, cross each other's paths as one section relieves the other. It meant that at that moment on that day there were at least twenty willing and able Coast Guard service members eager to be assigned to this SAR case. Walter could order all three boats of this one-boat station into action, manning each with four crew members and still leaving sufficient staff to man the home front.

But with the station commander out on the search, the home front at Montauk now became the responsibility of Boatswain's Mate Dennis Heard. He arrived on duty at 7:00 a.m., was filled in on the situation, and found himself in charge of the station and responsible for managing the SAR case as well as for all operational and personnel issues that might arise for that case or any other issue at the station. Like Jason Rodocker in New Haven, Heard was something of a newbie at Montauk; he had arrived from Virginia Beach only a couple of weeks before and was still getting his bearings, "trying to figure out where the mess deck was," he says with a grin—"mess deck" being Coast Guard lingo for cafeteria.

Unlike Rodocker, however, who would spend his day huddled over a computer generating emotion-free data, Heard was in the thick of it. This was Montauk, after all, home to both Aldridge and Sosinski and headquarters of the commercial fishing fraternity of which they were a part. With only a skeleton crew left on station, with no additional boats available to handle any other issues that might arise, and with a community that would soon surely stir itself into worried watchfulness, Heard, a veteran of numerous SAR cases, was about to experience a baptism by fire of a magnitude he could never have anticipated. For the moment, he took up residence in the glass-walled communications center in the windowless interior of the station's main building.

Meanwhile, in the New Haven command center's communications suite, Sean Davis continued to try to extract from a still-shaken Anthony Sosinski all he could to determine where Aldridge had fallen over. Anthony again recounts his story, as if telling it a second time will help him understand his own situation: "I'm being totally straight up with you here," he tells Davis. "I went to bed four to five miles off Montauk, 8:30 or 9:00, and he"—Johnny—"went on watch. My other crew member went to bed too, so John was the only one awake. And you know he fell over somewhere, and now I'm sixty miles offshore."

"What was he wearing?" Davis asks.

"Honestly," says Anthony, and you can hear the sob in his voice, "I don't know at this time."

"Is he a good swimmer?" asks Davis.

"Yes. Yes, he is," Sosinski replies. "He is in exceptionally good shape. He's very resourceful also."

But at just about the time he said that, Aldridge himself was floating, not swimming. He was trying to survey the horizon, when he could see it, because that thin line was the only other thing in his world right now besides a vast, churning body of water. If he could see the horizon, he might be able to think up some way to put to use whatever survival resources he had.

Chapter 5

Daylight

Approximately 6:30 a.m.

Here comes the sun, and I am not feeling the sweet vibes the song sings about. In fact, I am feeling more vulnerable than I did when I was covered in darkness. But it is daylight, and something is telling me that it's time to go, time to do something.

Find a buoy. That's a pretty straightforward but almost impossible task. For one thing, the sun's glare makes it almost impossible for me to see in any direction except north. Mostly, however, it's the waves that are keeping me from seeing anything.

The waves, the waves. I remind myself it isn't the water that's moving—it's energy, and that is what I will be going up against when I move. Right now I don't want to fight that energy. I just need to rise and fall to see what I can when I can. My chin is just about on the surface of the water, and as the waves lift me up, I get only a couple of seconds at the crest when I can see above the surface—my only chance for a sighting of the horizon. Then the waves take me down again and in the trough, I see only water.

For a long, long time I see nothing. I'm just bobbing, being carried, stretching my neck each time I rise. Nothing. Meanwhile, like any foreign body in the water, I have become a living ecosystem—the host to numerous guests. Sea lice, crustaceans, shrimp are all over my limp body. The storm petrels are dive-bombing me again. The taste of seawater is constant—I would kill for cool, fresh water to get the taste out of my mouth. I really want to move. I want to be moving. But should I? Is it safer, smarter, a better shot at survival to just drift, just wait? There's nothing to see. My neck has to strain for even a quick glimpse of the horizon, but I have yet to sight a buoy. I would love to find something—anything—to float on.

If I do swim when I see something to swim to, how will I do it? I think about that: *How should I propel myself?* I can't let go of my boots, which means that one arm will have to continue to hold onto them, leaving me only one arm to swim with—at a time, that is: I'll have to switch off from time to time. And most of the forward push will have to come from my kick—hard frog-kicking to move through these waves.

Then I catch, for an instant, a glimpse of Pete Spong's buoy. Pete is a friend, a colleague, a lobster fisherman out of Point Judith, Rhode Island. I know his gear almost as well as I know my own. And there it is, in my sight: the red float familiar, unmistakable, and beckoning.

I'm going. It's time. Past time: I figure it has been light for a while already—certainly an hour, maybe more. Time is not on my side.

I resupply the boots with air, one at a time, then hold them both close to my chest with my left arm, one in each armpit. I lie down a bit on the water, kick at the same time that I pull with my right arm, and I am on the move. It is hard work, made harder by the fact that I have to keep trying to get a visual of what I'm aiming for even as I labor to make headway. I push all that out of my mind: *Hard? So what? You swim or you die.*

Slow going. I swim a bit, then need to rest, switch hands, swim again, rest again. But I get a kind of rhythm: ten, maybe fifteen minutes of hard-core swimming, then hold up, relax. I'm working my way there, to Pete's buoy. I keep going, keep going. Half an hour of swimming. An hour maybe. One-armed swimming is not easy.

All of a sudden there is a fin almost three feet long right next to me, and my heart shoots out of my body. I hadn't expected to see sharks in daylight. Sharks at night, yes, but in daylight they head for deeper water. I feel this fish coming right up against me until it shoots upward and I am looking into the prehistoric face of an ocean sunfish. Weighing, at a minimum, five hundred pounds, the animal has a little round mouth and huge eyes and is said to be the heaviest bony fish in the ocean. I have seen ocean sunfish many times. I have watched them hurl their enormous round bodies out of the water in a leaping motion. They prey on jellyfish and are preyed on by sharks, but right now this one is interested in exploring *me*, and he has virtually fastened himself to my side to do so. I have to kick him a couple of times to make him go away, but he does, and I keep heading for the buoy.

I am definitely getting closer, but the work of swimming seems to be getting harder. I begin to ask myself if this is worth it, if this is the buoy I should be aiming for.

Maybe thirty yards away now—so close—and something has happened. Maybe the tide is picking up. Something! The sea has just become ripping here. I'm being swept off my hard-won course, away from the buoy, and clearly, in trying to get to it, I will lose so much energy that I will exhaust myself completely. I've been aiming for an east-end buoy—there's no flag on the highflyer!—but there is too much tide. I decide to give up. I realize I've wasted an hour of hard labor. But I need to cut my losses now and preserve what strength I have left to head for Pete's west-end buoy.

Okay. An hour of hard labor has eliminated one possibility. Time to reassess.

In fact, I have learned something important. I can see from here how the buoy is trailing in the current, which keeps pushing it west. The current is pushing me west as well. I hadn't even thought about that when I started swimming, but now it's so obvious. If I am going to get to the west-end buoy, I will actually need to swim northeast. I will need to get up ahead of the buoy so that I, pushed by the current, can fall down onto it.

That's what I've just learned: either I make use of the current or it will prevent me from getting where I'm going altogether.

So I try to rest my body and my brain too, try to calm my breathing, try to slow down the adrenaline. Soon I will start to look to the west for the buoy, and when I see it, I will swim to it. But not directly.

Meanwhile taking time to rest gives room for the terror and grief to come back into my head. I have got to quiet them down, and the only way I can do that is to reach for normalcy—something trivial, meaningless, even stupid. Right now the trivial, the meaningless, and the stupid are soothing, and I long for them. I grab onto a mental picture of the vacuum cleaner on the porch that I borrowed from my friend Pauly. What was it—a Eureka? a Hoover? a Bissell? Was it an upright? Was it a dirt devil? Was the bag pretty full when I borrowed it? Let me just concentrate on that, on the vacuum cleaner. It is comforting to focus on something so ordinary. It alleviates the fear, lifts the misery to remember vacuum cleaners and what they look like and how they work and the way they sweep up dirt and keep my apartment neat and clean. Vacuum cleaners are so normal and so far away from all this.

I hear a low-pitched shuddering sound overhead and somewhere in the distance. I look to the horizon, and I see it way up there: a tiny dot. A helicopter. I'm sure that's a helicopter. It means Anthony is awake and on it. They're looking for me.

I feel—something. Less alone, I think. Not so terrifyingly alone.

Chapter 6

In the Command Center

7:28 a.m.

Anthony Sosinski had gotten hold of himself. The man who had acknowledged to Sean Davis that he was "freaking out" and was "beside" himself now seemed composed and in control. Perhaps the steady stream of questions Davis had been asking, requiring precisely detailed answers, is what calmed him. Whatever it was, Sosinski was back in command of his boat and was focused on his present purpose: helping the US Coast Guard find Johnny.

The situation, as Anthony and the planners at New Haven understood it at seven that morning, was that Aldridge was last seen at about nine o'clock the previous evening, a time when the *Anna Mary* was approximately five nautical miles south of Montauk on a course of 180 magnetic and traveling at approximately six and a half knots. In landlubber terms the boat was going due south at a speed of about seven and a half miles an hour.

Because John was supposed to wake Anthony at 11:30 and did not, the thinking was that he had fallen into the water at some point between the hours of 9:00 and 11:30; otherwise, he would have awakened Anthony, right? So somewhere in that two-and-a-half-hour stretch is when he went overboard. Call that the starting point—the northern edge or top limit that might define where to search. The other limit, the end point at the southernmost edge, would be the point at which the *Anna Mary* had stopped and reversed course at around six this morning. Put these two facts together and you conclude that Johnny had fallen in at a spot somewhere between five nautical miles and sixty-plus nautical miles offshore—that is, somewhere in the area the *Anna Mary* traversed in the hours between nine the previous evening and six this morning.

As probable locations for a search go, that's a big area—in excess of 780 square miles—more than half the size of Rhode Island. If you're going to search an area of that size effectively, which was precisely the issue before the search mission participants in the New Haven command center that morning, you confront two basic questions: What kind of pattern do you draw across the area, and how do you best deploy the available assets in support of the search—assets consisting of both the search response units, the SRUs, with their crews and staff, and the resources available for deployment? And then, of course, all of that needs to be put together effectively in a coordinated and detailed search plan that SAROPS could continually update and correct.

Mission coordinator Jonathan Theel was frustrated from the outset. True, the appropriate first steps had been taken: the pan pan distress call had been broadcast and liaison had been established with Montauk Station and with Air Station Cape Cod. Assets from both were on their way to the probable search location. But a detailed, coordinated search plan had not yet been fully developed, and even though, as Theel himself says, "searching is an art as well as a science," for the man in overall command of the search, as he was, the slow pace at which SAROPS was being put to work was exasperating. Still, Theel well knew the difficulties the planning operation confronted—especially in this case, where there was minimal certainty about where John Aldridge had gone overboard or how long ago and therefore how to define the probable search area.

The first step for the planning team was to designate a search pattern. The Coast Guard is masterful at creating and assigning the right pattern out of a library of patterns devised to deal with a range of situations: a parallel pattern when the lost object could be anywhere in a large area, a creeping-line pattern when the lost object is likely to be in one end of the search area rather than the other, a sector-search pattern that looks like the spokes of a wheel for when the target is really difficult to see, a barrier-search when the current is strong, or a host of other patterns. But when you really don't have a lot of information to go on, when all you really know is the course the object was traveling when it got lost, then you order a trackline-search pattern, which is exactly what the Coast Guard did now, officially initiating what is called a trackline-search-and-return pattern, TSR.

They began by drawing a virtual box around the course the
Anna Mary had been traveling. At the midpoint of the top
line of the box, they established the latitude and longitude
of where the *Anna Mary* had been at nine o'clock the night
before, and at the midpoint of the bottom line of the box, they
noted the coordinates for the point when Anthony turned
around and reversed course at six in the morning. They determined that the search pattern would follow up and down
the line between those two points, looking to both sides.

At 7:16 a.m. the order was duly relayed to Station Montauk's forty-seven-foot motor lifeboat, already underway, to
start searching south at 180 magnetic until it reached twenty
nautical miles offshore. In essence, the lifeboat would start
where the *Anna Mary* had started and then head in the direction it had taken to Aldridge's and Sosinski's first line of traps,
with crew members looking to the left and to the right—to
east and to west.

At the same time the *Anna Mary* was doing the same thing
in reverse, running a trackline back to where it had started,
with Mike Migliaccio up on top looking to left and right, east
and west, and Anthony at the railing with the radio microphone in his hand doing the same.

But where should the MH-60 helicopter out of Air Station Cape Cod start to search? In the middle—between the
47 steaming south and the *Anna Mary* steaming north? And
what about the other assets being readied or getting underway—the cutters identified as available, the second boat—the
small response boat—out of Montauk Station, and a fixed-
wing aircraft as well? SAROPS is still at work churning out a

search plan specific to this event, so in the meantime how do the Coast Guard planners make best use of the assets to find this guy? Is there a way to figure out if he fell over closer to the top of the trackline, the coordinates at the five-nautical mile mark, or closer to the bottom of the trackline, at the sixty-plus nautical mile mark? And do they run the risk, with assets converging, that when everything between five miles and sixty miles is a priority, nothing is a priority?

These were some of the questions and issues that Jonathan Theel as search mission coordinator and the rest of the planning team wrestled with that morning, even as they were bent on both developing the needed information and devising the right plan for the search.

Theel zeroed in on that two-and-a-half-hour window between 9:00 and 11:30 p.m., between the last time anybody saw John and the time he was supposed to wake Anthony. That seemed critical to Theel, and he decided to run a quick weighting exercise through SAROPS. It convinced him to deploy 60 percent of the assets to the top of the trackline, closer to 9:00 p.m. and the five-mile mark, and 40 percent to the bottom of the trackline, where the *Anna Mary* would have been after 11:30. That weighting exercise would now be built out as part of developing the detailed search plans.

So at 7:28 that morning the MH-60 helicopter was ordered to start searching at a point five to ten nautical miles offshore, and it was probably just arriving there when John Aldridge spotted it as a dot on the far horizon.

Similar to the famed Army Blackhawk helicopter that gets in all the movies, the MH-60 helicopter is, for several reasons, particularly well suited to search-and-rescue operations. For one thing, it is big. The MH-60 carries two pilots plus two lookouts, one on each side, so there are more eyeballs on the water—*exclusively* on the water. It is loud too. The MH-60 can be heard by a survivor bobbing on the waves, and bobbing on the waves is precisely what John Aldridge was doing that very morning. And it can fly close to the water as well, which affords better visibility to both searchers and survivors.

On arrival at its starting point the MH-60 was further ordered to drop a datum, a self-locating data marking buoy, which could track actual set and drift in the area—that is, the direction in which the current was flowing and the speed at which it was moving, two factors of significance in trying to determine where a lost object might be.

Those factors were very much on the mind of John Aldridge, the lost object, who was reconsidering their effect on his ability to get where he wanted to go—conceivably at the exact moment he spotted that dot in the sky that was no doubt the MH-60.

The helicopter wasn't alone in the air. Air Station Cape Cod also sent out a fixed-wing aircraft, the HC-144 Ocean Sentry. This is a medium-range surveillance aircraft, able therefore to cover a lot of distance and sweep over a lot of territory, and it holds a profusion of advanced sensing and communications capabilities. The downside is that when the tail of the 144 is up, visibility out the windows is minimal; the tail needs to be lowered for the 144 to serve as an effective visual platform. But with the 144 and the multi-eyed MH-60 helicopter out there, John Aldridge's chances of being seen and rescued were certainly improved.[*]

Altogether, by 8:30 that morning two aircraft, a forty-seven-foot motor lifeboat, and a twenty-five-foot response boat were all out looking for John Aldridge on the trackline-search pattern plotted in New Haven, and the two cutters, the *Tiger Shark* and the *Sailfish*, were being prepared to join them.

By this time Mark Averill, a veteran of the service now operating in a civilian capacity and serving today as command duty officer, CDO, had determined to make use of the technology-proficient Jason Rodocker to operate the SAROPS system, freeing Pete Winters, another civilian, to liaise over the communications lines with Sosinski as well as with personnel on other fishing vessels now coming online.

The Coast Guard's use of retired veterans returning in civilian capacities is one of the service's more interesting and astute features. The civilians may work as much as eighty hours over a two-week period, attend retraining to maintain or gain proficiency in various skills, and bring to their assignments both experience and a certain maturity. They also "provide continuity," says Mark Averill, imbuing the immediacy of a day like July 24, 2013, with institutional memory—a profound

---

[*] At 10:08 a.m. a Good Samaritan private aircraft piloted by retired Army Lieutenant Colonel George Drago, active with the USCG Auxiliary, received USCG clearance to join the search, albeit at a different altitude from the fixed-wing 144 and the MH-60. Drago had been alerted to the emergency by Chuck Weimer and Bill Grimm, both captains of commercial fishing vessels, who joined him on the flight. The plane malfunctioned before reaching the search area and had to return to the Montauk airport.

but also intuitive knowledge of how the service works and what it can do. Averill's shuffling of Rodocker and Winters embodies the kind of value a civilian can offer: Rodocker, who had grown up in the era of computing and instant Internet access, was a proven expert at wielding SAROPS's multiple inputs and capabilities; he had honed his skills during his term in Baltimore, where the natural abundance of rivers and streams makes for what Rodocker calls "multiple search areas," giving him plenty of practice in "cases with multiple scenarios in one drift"—something, he says, "I know how to do." Winters was admittedly less practiced in SAROPS subtleties, but he is a commercial fisherman as well as a veteran of the Coast Guard, a man familiar with the fishing grounds off Montauk, and it was thought that because he and Anthony spoke the same fisherman's language, he might be able to learn more and keep Anthony focused. That proved to be exactly right.

Anthony had not left his post. He continued to serve as both the in-charge first source for information and as the primary advocate asking for every asset the Coast Guard could muster, plus help from every ship, fishing vessel, yacht, or dinghy he could connect with in the high-frequency radio world. He did this even as he was wearing out his own eyes staring at the sea while standing precariously on the railing of the *Anna Mary*—shirtless, shoeless, sweating from head to toe, his very *feet* sweating, as he remembers it, tied to the radio via a long line.

He was also, in equal parts, terrified and sick at heart. His cocaptain, his business partner, his pal from age seven, his brother from another mother was somewhere out there in the great ocean, alone. As to whether Johnny was dead or alive, he just didn't let himself go there.

Instead, he kept his mind churning. Everything he laid his eyes on, every communication with any of the growing crowd of fishermen rallying to search for Johnny became a potential clue, another bit of intelligence for the Coast Guard search planners, another possible building block of rescue. He heard from a scallop-boat captain out of New Bedford, Massachusetts, who "thought" the *Anna Mary* had gone around his stern at about 2:00 a.m. in thirty-two fathoms of water—two hundred feet—at the Loran position of 43 640. If accurate—if it *was* the *Anna Mary* and not one of the several other fishing vessels in the area at that time—it could have meant Johnny was alive and onboard well later than 9:00 p.m. and farther offshore than originally thought: even with autopilot, it usually requires someone on watch to dodge around a sudden obstacle on the autopilot track. Anthony duly reported that sighting to the Coast Guard. He also noted that Johnny's fishing skins were still on the boat—the waterproof garments that are a fisherman's work clothes. That told him that Johnny wouldn't have been dealing with bait, because if he had, he would have "dressed" for the job in the skins. He reported that to the Coast Guard as well. Other things he came upon— the bottle of eye drops Johnny was supposed to take for his glaucoma—sent him into a new tailspin of grief. At one point he found himself yelling at Johnny's driver's license, left out on the wheelhouse dashboard. "Where the hell are you?!" he screamed at the photo.

One good thing was that right away he and the Coast Guard's Pete Winters had connected with one another, mainly because Winters could "speak" Loran, the old Long Range Navigation system developed during World War II. Loran determines position by measuring the difference between two sets of signal pulses transmitted from two widely separated stations, and it expresses the measurement as the rate of the pulses' duration in microseconds. Although Loran has been supplanted in the military by the far more precise GPS, the global positioning navigation system based on satellite measurements, it remains the staple of the commercial fishing community—"not a perfect system," in Anthony's phrase, but the system in which commercial fishermen have defined their lanes and set their gear, so still universally relevant in that community. It meant a lot that he and Winters shared the Loran vocabulary, and it meant even more that Winters knew the waters where Anthony and Johnny fished. Anthony could talk to the Coast Guard in his own terms, knowing he was understood.

If Anthony had a single aim that morning, it was to shrink the search area where both he and the Coast Guard were looking. Data was flowing into his brain at much the same rate at which it flowed into the Coast Guard's computers, and that data was being weighed and measured by the instruments of Anthony's own vast experience and natural savvy about the ocean, about fishermen, about Johnny. There were observations that seemed significant—the speed and direction of the swells, for example, which can vary depending on what piece of ocean real estate you occupy: at the piece of real estate Anthony occupied at the time, the ocean was drifting to the northwest, while the Coast Guard, which had dropped its marking buoys farther inshore, was basing its calculations on a northeast drift.

There were other facts or suppositions that had to be discarded, although not before he had thought them through. Pete Spong called him about items he pulled out of the flotsam and jetsam drifting not far from his gear—a bushel basket with orange twine, a blue rubber glove of the kind lobstermen use to haul their catch out of traps, a cardboard box. If they were from the *Anna Mary*, they might help pinpoint the location where Johnny had fallen in. And yes! Johnny and Anthony used baskets of that description to haul ice onto the boat—maybe Johnny had lowered one into the water to scoop up something, tripped, and fallen in. But without a precise count of the number of baskets they had on board, Anthony could not determine whether the floater was one of theirs, so that "clue" proved unreliable. The blue glove, as it turned out, was a different brand from the kind used on the *Anna Mary*, so toss that one, and the cardboard box was not the same kind as those used on the *Anna Mary* to haul bait. Toss that one as well.

But Anthony kept putting the pieces together as if he were working a jigsaw puzzle, testing each datum in the crucible of his knowledge and experience and discarding what didn't work. Then, a little before 8:30 in the morning, his brain lit up with the answer.

The key was in something Pete Spong told him. Pete reported that he woke up the night before at around 4:00 a.m.

on his boat, the *Brooke C*, drank some coffee, recognized the distinctive lights of the *Anna Mary* moving past in the distance—a boat's lights can be its signature in the night—and at about 4:30 a.m. radioed over for a friendly chat. Pete remembers thinking that it was a little bit odd to see the *Anna Mary* going by at that time, but he figured that because it was pretty breezy out, Anthony and Johnny were waiting for morning to start hauling their traps. His radio call was not answered.

This told Anthony that Johnny absolutely was not in the wheelhouse at that time, 4:30 a.m., for he certainly would have answered Pete if he had been available and able to do so.

Because, according to Spong, the *Brooke C* had been at the Loran position of 43 565 at 4:30 a.m. and because Johnny hadn't answered the call, there was no point searching south of that line. That meant that the bottom line of the search area, as earlier calculated, was too far south. The original calculation had put the bottom of the search area at the moment of Anthony's first radio call to the Coast Guard, when he was in a state of stunned stupor—at the 420 line, the southernmost point considered as a search area boundary.

After a while Anthony also realized that of course Johnny would have stopped the *Anna Mary* as soon as it arrived at its projected first trawl, somewhere around the 515 line. He would have roused Anthony and Mike so they could all start hauling up traps. That was standard operating procedure, and because it hadn't happened, Johnny was clearly already off the boat by the 515 line. The additional fact learned from Pete—that Johnny hadn't been on the boat to answer the call from Pete at the 565 line—in essence narrowed the search track by another fifty microseconds.

The *Anna Mary*'s rate of travel was yet another confirming factor in the equation, for at its speed of just over six knots per hour, it would have taken just about an hour for the boat to travel those fifty microseconds of positional difference.

Add it all up: Pete's 4:30 a.m. call, the *Brooke C*'s position at the time he made the call, Pete thinking it was odd that the *Anna Mary* passed by when it did, and another possible hour of travel, and the sum-total conclusion is that Johnny could easily have fallen off the boat north of the 565 line.

The conclusion effectively lopped five miles off the bottom boundary of the probable search location. It may not sound like much, but when you're searching an area the size of about twenty-five Manhattan Islands, every microsecond counts.

Anthony was putting together other clues as well, sharpening his mental picture of what had happened. He remembered that when he and Mike Migliaccio had first gone out on deck to search for Johnny, in those frightening first moments when they confronted the idea of him being gone, Anthony had seen that both pumps were on—both the fill tank and the discharge tank pumps, that the discharge cap was on the starboard tank while the port tank was closed with no cap—meaning that it was discharging water, that the coolers weren't where they were supposed to be, and that one of the cooler handles had broken off. His first thought was that Johnny had decided to fill the tanks early to weigh down the boat a little bit—there was a "lazy swell" in the ocean that night—part of that same weather condition Pete Spong had described as breezy. Filling the tanks could help steady the *Anna Mary* to make for a more comfortable ride.

But what if Johnny had stayed awake for some other reason? The reason Anthony had in mind now was that Johnny might have been carrying out the plan the two of them had agreed upon the day before. The plan was based on their understanding that their recently installed refrigeration system cooled the water at a rate of about four degrees an hour. So the two men had determined that the best time to fill the tanks and then start the cooling was two hours before they reached their traps at the 515 line—probably somewhere around 3:00 or 3:30 a.m. The navigational marker for that point in time was where the *Anna Mary* typically reached the forty-fathom curve—where the ocean depth reaches 240 feet—at the 600 line. So, in Anthony's words, they would start filling tanks "no sooner than the 600 line so we give ourselves a good two hours to chill the water down." What he now found himself speculating was that Johnny was getting ready to fill the tanks and got interrupted in midtask. Anthony even visualized—and was absolutely correct in his visualization—what had happened to cause the interruption. He stepped out on deck, zeroed in on the coolers, and noted the broken handle on the bottom one. The clarity was electric.

Anthony radioed Pete Winters at the Coast Guard command center and told him what he now felt certain he knew. "At this time," he said to Winters, "I believe that John did fall over at somewhere in the vicinity of the 43 600 line." As

Winters understood at once, this was a point considerably farther south than originally thought and that, in turn, substantively narrowed the size of the probable search area.

"Looks like he slid the cooler back," Anthony told the Coast Guard, "the handle broke off, and he went off the back of the boat. That's what it appears at this time."

"Roger. Good copy, captain," came the reply from New Haven.

Anthony had nailed it. Johnny hadn't fallen over before 11:30 but some hours after that time—probably in the wee hours of the morning, at the top of forty fathoms of depth and somewhere in the 600s on Loran.

In the command center in New Haven, aided by Pete Winters's fluency in "fisherman talk," Jonathan Theel now ordered the watch to begin rerunning SAROPS, shifting the 60–40 north-south weighting exactly the other way, with the greater weight of assets now focusing on the southern end of the estimated trackline.

Meanwhile SAROPS had run what is called a survivability simulation—a key element in the planning process because it lets the SAR planners know how much time they may have to be planning for. Clothing can play a role in survivability, which is why Sean Davis had asked Anthony what Johnny had been wearing when he fell over, a question Anthony had been unable to answer.

The simulation spits out two models: functional time and survivable time. Functional time quantifies the extent to which a person lost in the ocean can use most of the body's big muscles—it's about the ability to swim. Survivable time means how long you can keep your head above water. The SAROPS calculation determined that the best-case survivability scenario for fit, five-foot-nine, 150-pound John Aldridge was that he could probably stay afloat for nineteen hours before succumbing to hypothermia and/or fatigue. The functional model—his ability to use his big arm and leg muscles and, therefore, to swim—was considerably shorter; it was also much more difficult to calculate without knowing more about Johnny Aldridge's condition at the time he went overboard. The guessing, however, was that his functional survivability was more like five or six hours. Coast Guard planners also know well that an individual's will to live can influence these simulation results, which are meant only to offer a quantifying framework for planning. The problem is that no one has yet come up with an algorithm that can either measure the will to live or predict how it will manifest itself.

In John Aldridge at that moment the will to live was manifesting itself as a determination to propel his body through the ocean toward the west-end buoy of Pete Spong's line of lobster traps.

But Jonathan Theel had no way of knowing that when he turned to the next task at hand on the mission coordinator's checklist: the very tough task of informing the Aldridge family that John was missing.

Chapter 7

"We're in Big Trouble"

9:15 a.m.

John Aldridge II was working in the garage that morning, as he often did. He keeps a workshop there and fixes and tunes the equipment his son Anthony uses in his landscaping business. Aldridge is an incurable fixer-upper. His daughter, Cathy, complains lovingly that "nothing gets thrown out—he will fix everything."

The ringing cell phone barely broke his stride. As is his habit, he looked at the number of the caller and, since he didn't recognize it, did not interrupt his work to answer but let it go to voicemail. Fifteen minutes later, when he had finished what he was doing, he listened to the message and took down the number for the return call.

It was Commander Somebody-or-other from the Coast Guard. Aldridge has his own boat that is registered with the Coast Guard, and he assumed there was some problem with the renewal paperwork for the registration. When he got through to the Coast Guard he was told that "the commander would like to speak with you, please hold." He hung on for a few minutes, reviewing in his mind the various registration forms and trying to determine which one he hadn't filled out properly—there couldn't be any other reason for the call— and then Jonathan Theel got on the phone.

Theel had substantial experience making calls of this nature. He reckons that in the space of a year he is called upon to inform families of things they don't want to hear anywhere from half a dozen to a dozen times—"unfortunately," as he puts it, "way too many times." He prepares by learning what he can about the person he is calling and by gathering all the information available on the person he is reporting on. In this case the available information on the missing John Aldridge was minimal. Theel also rehearses in his head how he will begin—by introducing himself, explaining who he is, stating the facts, and outlining what the US Coast Guard is doing about the situation. It is never easy.

"I have some bad news for you," Theel said after his preamble, and Aldridge felt his knees give way. "Your son John is missing at sea."

The first picture that flashed across Aldridge's mind was that of his son in the water and tangled in the propeller. He asked Theel: "How? Did he get caught in a line?"

"We don't know," the commander replied. "We only know he's not on the boat. He went overboard sometime before sunup, but we don't know when. We don't know how long he's been missing." He added that Coast Guard assets were out looking for John—a crew launched out of Station Montauk and aircraft were en route from Cape Cod.

Theel asked whether Aldridge wanted to "have Mrs. Aldridge get on another extension," but Aldridge said no. Instead, he walked upstairs with the phone still at his ear and Theel still on the line. He wanted to tell her himself, but he wanted Theel there as well.

Addie was in the kitchen.

"We're in big trouble," John said.

Her hand automatically covered her mouth. She thought, *He's been down in the garage—he cut himself on some machine.*

"What?" she demanded. "What?"

"It is the Coast Guard calling about Johnny," John said, and Addie began to crumble. John told her what he knew, repeated the information Theel again offered in his ear, and gathered himself sufficiently to thank Theel and to ask him to "please keep us informed." Then he telephoned his other children.

Cathy Patterson was at home that morning with her husband, Tommy, who had worked the night shift at his job as a deputy sheriff in Suffolk County, and her son, Jake, four years old at the time. They were all upstairs in the colonial-style house. It was early morning in summertime, and as the song has it, the livin' was easy. Tommy and Jake were in Jake's room, Jake still in his pajamas, watching cartoons on TV from Jake's bed. She could hear them laughing as she turned off the shower and stepped out of the tub. She threw on a T-shirt and a pair of shorts and was just about to blow dry her bright blond hair when the phone rang. She heard at once in her father's voice that something was terribly wrong. He sounded "wrecked," distraught.

"The Coast Guard called and said Johnny's missing," John Aldridge told his daughter. The blow nearly knocked her over.

"Missing? He's missing?"

From his room just off the hallway her young son heard her end of the call. Jake knew what his uncle did for a living and sensed something terribly wrong. No surprise there: Johnny and Jake are two halves of a mutual adoration society and share a special kinship.

"Did Uncle Johnny fall in the water?" Jake now asked his mother. Tommy stood behind him, a hand on his son's shoulder. He too was stunned.

Cathy nodded, *Yes.* It was all she could manage.

"Are there sharks in the water?"

She nodded again.

"Will the Coast Guard save him?"

"Yes," Cathy said. "And I am going to go to Montauk to get him."

She had to see to her parents first. Their house, where she and Johnny and their kid brother, Anthony, had grown up, was two minutes by car from her own home. People who grow up in Oakdale tend not to move far away. Her mother was seated and in tears. Her father was pacing. She suspected that in his mind his son was dead and buried.

Her brother Anthony and his wife, Jillian, walked in a few moments later. Anthony had been at work on his truck when his father called him, breaking the news to his youngest child as he had to his wife. "We have a problem," he said to Anthony. "Your brother is missing, and it's not good." Anthony Aldridge, although the baby of the family, is a big, burly man, but he is also a man in whom emotions lie close to the surface. At his father's words he broke apart. Like his father, he felt a sudden emptiness in the world. He had often fished with his brother; he knew this could happen in a heartbeat. Now he felt at once that Johnny was gone and saw the loss extending throughout his own lifetime. Too distraught to drive, he asked one of his workers to drive him home.

Only Cathy seemed to be holding it together. "I go into business mode," she says of herself. She reminded herself that Jillian, by nature gentle and caring, was also a nurse who could bring professional expertise to bear to steady a stressful situation. *Thank God*, Cathy thought. She asked her father exactly what the Coast Guard commander had said. Just that there had been a "distress call from Anthony Sosinski, that he woke up and Johnny was gone." Right now there was nothing more to learn.

"I have to go to the Coast Guard station in Montauk," said Cathy. It was decided that Jillian would go with her. The relationship between the sisters-in-law is a tight one, as is that between Jillian and her brother-in-law. Johnny is the big brother she never had in the same way that she is the sister Cathy never had, and Jillian is also acutely aware of the important role Johnny plays in her husband's life. The thought of him endlessly treading water, if he were still alive and uninjured, was painful. She also knew that Cathy, tough as she is, should not face whatever had to be faced on her own.

So Anthony would man the home front with his parents and would try to hold things together. The two women would simply install themselves at the Coast Guard station and not leave until Johnny was found—as no one wanted to say aloud—dead or alive.

"You bring my son home to me," her mother said to Cathy as she walked out the door. "Please, Cathy. Bring my Johnny home."

"I will," she vowed.

There are advantages to being married to a deputy sheriff, Tommy Patterson's rank at the time. One of them is that the sheriff's department has its own marine bureau, which was itself gearing up to respond in any way possible to the loss of local lobsterman Johnny Aldridge. The bureau gave Cathy and Jillian an escort, so the seventy-plus-mile drive, which usually takes at least an hour and a half, two hours if there's traffic, took only fifty minutes. During the drive Cathy watched her cell phone light up with texts and phone messages. The word was out.

There was no way for it not to be. VHF radio channel 16 is the standard marine communication channel, its chatter accessible to all ships required to carry radio as well as to radio towers in numerous coastal areas. Anyone at a listening post knew what was going on. Police scanner buffs, amateur radio operators, anyone with a plugin on a computer could hear what was happening and pass the news along.

Tony Vincente didn't hear the news from a computer or a VHF radio; he learned about Johnny in an urgent call from Johnny's brother, Anthony, and he was the first person outside the family to get the news. That's probably not surprising: Vincente has been a close friend of the whole family for a long time. Addie Aldridge babysat for Vincente's daughters, and Johnny himself, ten years Tony's junior, had worked for Vincente's construction firm as a carpenter and foreman. The call came while Vincente was at work on a job, a place where, it is well known, he does not like to be disturbed by personal phone calls. At the end of this one he walked off the job and went to his office to try to get hold of himself.

Then Lucy Catalano walked in the door. A close friend of Johnny's—the two had grown up together as neighbors in Oakdale—she had last spoken with him the evening before, phoning him at nine o'clock to announce that friends had arrived from Italy to spend their honeymoon in the States and were looking forward to seeing him. "I'm just pulling out of the slip," Johnny told her from aboard the *Anna Mary*. "I'll be back day after tomorrow and see all of you then." That morning Lucy took her guests to the beach at Robert Moses State Park. She was just unfolding the beach chairs when her phone rang—another friend, who had heard it from Tony, telling her that Johnny was missing. The news was both unfathomable and numbing. Somehow the beach chairs got refolded. Lucy and the Italian honeymooners got back in the car. She drove through Oakdale, and when she passed Vincente's office she pulled up to the curb, turned off the engine, and asked the honeymooners to wait. Tony was another link in the Johnny chain, and she felt the urge to see him.

Lucy walked in and saw Tony sobbing at his desk. She went over and embraced him, and the two of them hugged, weeping, for a long moment. Then he looked up at Lucy and said, "You know, our friend is not a strong swimmer."

Lucy couldn't take anymore. "I gotta go," she said. She brought her guests home, went into the hairdressing salon she runs out of her home, and got to work. It was the only thing she could think of to do with herself. Fortunately, she had a fully booked schedule of appointments for that day, although half of them—mostly Johnny's friends—had left messages canceling.

Meanwhile Tony Vincente picked himself up and went to the Aldridge house.

So did Steve D'Amico, who also got a call from Anthony. D'Amico had grown up across the street from the Aldridges—John and Addie Aldridge were "a second father and mother." He had to be with them.

Others were gathering. A line of cars was parked along the street as neighbors and friends began to dribble in, then to pour in, until what Cathy Patterson would later measure as "half of Oakdale" was at the house at the end of Yale Avenue.

The other half, like Cathy, was on its way to Montauk.

Chapter 8

"Johnny Load
Is Missing"

6:45 a.m.

Dead empty for most of the year, Montauk from June to September blossoms into Partytown, USA. Watch the crowds filing off the trains on a Friday evening in summer—unkindly locals have dubbed these conveyances "cattle cars"—or pouring out of jitneys from Manhattan and Brooklyn. They have arrived at what a reporter for the *New York Times* Fashion & Style section described in 2016 as "the former fishing village that's now a summer playground."* Forget the dismissive

---

* Caitlin Keating, "Keeping Montauk Mellow," *New York Times*, New York edition, August 25, 2016.

"former" for now—a playground it certainly is. Chic, glamorous, pricey, seductive, hot in any number of ways: that is Montauk in the summer, although if you needed just one word to describe the time and place, unarguably the word would be *crowded*.

One reason Montauk draws so many people is that its setting is unspeakably beautiful. True, it is dead flat. Although the nature preserve you ride through on your way to the town center and the Point boasts a peak elevation of 151 feet above sea level, for the most part you're standing just at sea level. That is one reason the 110-foot-high lighthouse, perched on a headland known as Turtle Hill at an elevation of a mere 71 feet, stands out so prominently. In fact, however, sea level affords long and wonderful vistas—north across white sand beaches to the harbors and bays of Long Island Sound and, in a simple pivot, south across dunes to the open Atlantic. There are fresh ponds, lush woods and gardens, lanes of traditional gray-shingled houses, sunrise walks past bass fishermen surf-casting in the near dark, evening sunsets over the harbor with the yachts and sailboats and charter boats and working fishing vessels more or less at rest but rocking ever so gently on the lapping tide. Little wonder that the people who love Montauk love it so fiercely, and little wonder the visitors cannot stay away.

Not that anyone really knows the exact number of people who visit here between Memorial Day and Labor Day, the traditional beginning and end of "the season." The Suffolk County Planning Commission claimed in 2015, as reported in the local *Easthampton Star* newspaper, that the number of people spending the night in the stretch of hamlets comprising the Hamptons and Montauk went from an estimated peak of 200,000 in 1990 to 262,000 in 2010.* That peak has almost surely been topped since then, as the appeal of the place as a pop-up summer resort has only increased, while new, online sites like Airbnb have augmented the possibilities for spending the night and have no doubt added unknown numbers to the total.

For a hamlet with an official population of not quite 4,000 and a population density of some 220 people per square mile, Montauk's share of these peak numbers, even if they are only estimates, is staggering.

The first to arrive are almost invariably the summertime residents, homeowners of long standing, who show up at the first signs of spring to air out their shuttered houses, turn on the pump and water heater, and start their gardens. Montaukers in their way, they will spend the summer months mostly with each other, secure in their status as old Montauk hands who know their way around.

Then there are the renters, those looking for a week or a month or a few nights in a house or cabin or condo or efficiency apartment or whatever they can find. The official kick-off for finding one of these is Presidents' Day in February, but the cognoscenti start even earlier—in many cases as far back as the previous November.

---

* David E. Rattray, "How Many Are Here? No One Knows," *Easthampton Star*, August 6, 2015, http://easthamptonstar.com/Living/2015806/How-Many-Are-Here-No-One-Knows.

Montauk is rich in hotels as well—from luxury spa resorts at top prices down to cheap motels with paper-thin walls. All are booked virtually all season long.

So is the stretch of shore known as Gin Beach—so named not, as many suppose, because the bootleggers offloaded cases of the stuff here during Prohibition but rather because this was the spot where, as far back as 1665, cattle and sheep were enclosed in summer behind a gate or corral known as a gin. Today the beach plays host to what the locals call Tin Can Caravan, a mass of parked RVs and camper trailers that can stay for up to a week at a stretch—for way less money than in an inn or B&B or hotel or motel.

Owners, renters, campers, and everybody else arrives from somewhere farther west on the train or the jitney, where the partying often begins en route, or in cars or vans that on weekends inch the last fifty miles at a snail's pace. They even arrive by helicopter—you can order one on an Uber-like app if you don't have your own.

What do all these people do when they get to Montauk? Of course, they play in the ocean. They swim, they bodysurf, they surf and paddleboard off the famous Ditch Plains Beach. They sail. They charter boats and go out for a day of deep-sea fishing, and if they get a strike, they might take a selfie with their catch.

They eat. Celebrity chefs make their way here with the summer crowds, purveying a variety of creative cuisines. As of the 2016 season, for example, as reported in the *New York Times*, diners could feast on "vegan dishes inspired by

Australian surf towns, like cantaloupe gazpacho with egg-plant 'bacon' and borage."*

They drink. They imbibe copious amounts of rosé and other wines, microbrews and Budweisers, liquor and cordials, and, famously, the Fireball Shot, consisting of a tossed-back shot of the famous whisky chased by a pint of hard cider.

They shop. In addition to the usual tourist sweatshirts and baseball caps, you can pay a fortune for a beach cover-up at any number of fashionable boutiques or at the summer outposts of trendy Manhattan chains.

And they make noise. On Friday the singles arrive, and after a week cooped up in office buildings in the steamy city, they are really, really ready to release their inhibitions and extend the range of the possible when it comes to their definition of fun. On occasion the all-night noise that results has generated contention and confrontation between residents and partyers, and that has become an issue in local politics. But the singles still come, and the parties go on.

That is Montauk in the summer. It's the Montauk you read about, the Montauk of lavish, A-list parties where you can spot celebrities like Alec Baldwin, Billy Joel, Steven Spielberg, and Taylor Swift. It is the Montauk everybody knows, the high-end world that gossip columnists have probed and social commentators have analyzed.

---

* Caitlin Keating, "A Guide to Your Summer in the Hamptons," *New York Times*, May 25, 2016, www.nytimes.com/2016/05/26/fashion/summer-party-eat-hamptons.html.

But it is not the real Montauk. Not even in summer. The real Montauk is about the fishing. It always was.

The town took its name from the Montaukett people who were the area's first inhabitants. They subsisted on what they fished and exchanged quahog clamshells as currency. Local historians think their hunting proficiency extended to trailing and killing whales from their dugout canoes, and it is certain that they made use of every bit of the animal, burning the whale oil in yet more clamshells. The Montaukett may even have taught whaling to European settlers when they arrived.

The place has been a fishing village ever since, and fishing is still the engine of the Montauk economy. The place is home to the largest commercial and recreational fishing fleet in New York state, one of the largest on the Eastern seaboard—and this despite the fact that the small commercial operations like that of the *Anna Mary*, long a mainstay of the economy, have been decimated by the regulations and quotas Johnny and Anthony and others complain about. Many of the fishermen who survived the regulations and limits did so by doubling up as sport-fishing operations, running those charter trips in summer for the tourists who want to tussle with bluefish, blackfish, striped bass, porgies, tuna, fluke. The claim that Montauk has more world saltwater fishing records than any other port remains unchallenged.

Locals like to say that when you get to Montauk, you've reached The End. That's literally true. You've reached the easternmost point of Long Island, which, at 118 miles in length, is the longest and largest island in the contiguous

United States. Running northeastward from New York Harbor and the city itself, Long Island on the map really does look like a fish swimming nose-first into the mainland, with a split tail in the east where Peconic Bay cuts the island into north and south peninsular forks. The south fork juts out farther than the north, and its East End is *The* End.

On this unlikely protrusion of dead-flat land sticking out from the indentation of the eastern seaboard, unlikely things have happened. The schooner *La Amistad* came ashore here in 1839, and the mutineers aboard, ethnic Mende men and women plucked from Africa to be sold in Caribbean slave markets, would take their case all the way to the Supreme Court to win their freedom, which they did.

During Prohibition Montauk was indeed a drop-off point for rum runners to stash their contraband, and in World War II almost the whole of the East End became a military base, its buildings disguised to look from above like a New England seaside village. Apparently non-New-England Montauk as it appeared at the time didn't quite fit the picture the military was after.

The lighthouse, standing on that headland at the easternmost end of Montauk Point, is a white tower with a distinctive red band. Unlike so many things that have assumed the description, it really is "iconic"—an essential part of the picture that is featured endlessly in logos, on postcards, and in selfies, sketches, drawings, paintings, and advertisements. A national historic landmark, it was commissioned by President George Washington in 1792, opened for business in 1796, and in one form or another has been there ever since.

For good reason. The piece of ocean the lighthouse over-looks is a dangerous spot. Here, where the deep Atlantic meets the mainland, below the windblown dunes where only beach grass grows, the rocky reefs and dangerous shoals are utterly exposed. When the waves roll against the tide, they rise up like towers and turn the inshore rip currents white with foam. More than one ship has foundered here, with the loss of all aboard. So once out of the narrow gate of the snug, closely protected Montauk Harbor, those heading out to sea—like Johnny and Anthony and their colleagues—know they are facing a rough and potentially dangerous ride around the Point before they can reach their own fishing grounds and their traps. In case they forget, there's an eight-foot, twenty-six-hundred-pound bronze statue of a fisherman standing atop a seven-foot-high block of granite at the lighthouse. It is a memorial, inscribed with the names of East End fishermen lost at sea—120 so far.

Anthony Sosinski is well acquainted with that memorial. In fact, he feels a particular connection with it. In March 1993 Anthony was working for a one-armed codfish captain named Pete on a boat called the *Some Pair*. Pete's limita-tion meant that he needed someone strong aboard to haul the gear, and wiry Anthony, corded with muscles, fit the bill. The two were on their way to head out on a scheduled trip when they made an early-morning stop to drop off a life raft for a friend of Pete's, a young fisherman named Joe Hodnik, who had just bought a longline boat for cod fishing and was about to take it on its maiden voyage with his friend and col-league Ed Sabo. Anthony and Pete stopped at Hodnik's home

and wished Hodnik well—Anthony remembers taking care
to keep his voice down because Hodnik's baby son, not yet
a year old, was asleep at the time—then headed out to sea.
Hodnik and Sabo did the same.

The *Some Pair* was off Block Island, and it was Anthony's
turn to keep watch during the nighttime drifting when, at
about 2:00 a.m., there came a distress call from Joe Hodnik shouting for Pete, giving out his Loran coordinates, and
screaming, literally, that he was sinking. Another boat, the
Provider, also heard the call and managed to send out the first
distress alert to the US Coast Guard and to broadcast Hodnik's coordinates. By the time Anthony and Pete on the *Some
Pair* got to the spot, a Coast Guard helicopter was circling
overhead. Anthony remembers how its brilliant searchlight
lit up the pitch-black ocean. The *Some Pair* pulled over to
where the deck box, empty now, was floating in the water.
They also found a boot and a toothbrush. The boat had gone
down quickly, and neither Joe Hodnik, twenty-six years old,
nor young Ed Sabo was ever found. Anthony is certain he was
the last human to hear Hodnik scream for help.

The loss of Joe Hodnik and Ed Sabo galvanized the Montauk fishing community to form the Lost At Sea Memorial
Committee in 1994, and when the memorial was dedicated
in 1999, the little boy Anthony hadn't wanted to wake up was
there, eight years old by then, to read his father's name in the
three-tiered base of the monument.

The sinking, the deaths, and the ringing memory of Joe's
final plea in Anthony's ears did something else: they prompted
Anthony to quit fishing altogether. *No more!* he decided.

He hung up his fisherman's skins and his heavy fisherman's boots, gathered his wife and child, and fled to Pennsylvania— far away from the sea and fish and everything having to do with either. He came back after a while, but not to Montauk and in no way to go out on the water; instead, he settled in Southampton and stayed away from boats. He made use of his professional expertise by going to work for the local King Kullen supermarket as a fish salesman—let somebody else go out there and risk their lives every day. He joined the union, the United Food and Commercial Workers International, and decided he had made the smartest move of his life.

But he couldn't stay away. Not from fishing and not from Montauk. And after nine months ashore and stuck indoors selling fish, he was back in the East End and back at sea.

What is telling about this is what it says about the hold the life of a fisherman can exert on an individual. Part of that hold surely is the protectively encompassing embrace of the Montauk fishing community—with all the support it offers and all the solidarity it lets its members feel. No doubt every profession or job is a fraternity—machinists, teachers, lawyers, construction workers, even bankers, for all anyone knows. They are fraternities of people who are fluent in a particular work-related jargon and who depend equally on a shared self-interest. The band of brothers that is the Montauk fishing community is that and more—a collective way of life that the community senses is under siege, such that everyone in the community has everyone else's back to the max. It's no accident and no surprise, for example, that little Joey Hodnik is today what his father before him was—a commercial fisherman—and an integral part of the Montauk fishing community.

Nor do you have to be a fisherman to be part of the community. George Watson, who runs The Dock, is no fisherman. Neither are the bartenders at Liar's, another "headquarters" of the fishing community. Cathy Patterson isn't a commercial fisherman either—nor is her husband Tommy, nor do they live in Montauk. Yet all are part of the Montauk fishing community. So is Jason Walter, the Coast Guard officer in charge of station Montauk at the time of the search for Johnny Aldridge. Two years later Walter retired from the service after a twenty-one-year career, and although he had spent only the last four of those years in Montauk, he and his family stayed on. This was home. Walter by this time knew virtually all the captains of all the fishing vessels, both sport and commercial, and he was to all of them a known quantity as well, a man who understood their struggles and their way of life, a man who had consistently gone above and beyond to help them and serve their interests. That Jason Walter, born and raised in the Pocono Mountains of Pennsylvania, was a brother in the fishing community was universally understood and accepted by every member of that community.

After his retirement from the service, Walter went to work at the Lighthouse on the Point, where he was daily aware of the tourists streaming to the Lost At Sea Memorial on which the name of Joey Hodnik's father is permanently incised. But he also understood what the memorial means to the fishermen of Montauk who pass it every day, every trip out to sea and home again. For them the memorial is both palpable evidence of their community's culture and heritage and an alarm bell telling them to remember the ever-present peril that's out there beyond the Point. The peril is inevitable, and it is part, at least, of what holds their community together and gives Montauk its edge, a sharp fisherman's intensity that residents say makes the place unlike any other.

Singer-songwriter Nancy Atlas has thought a lot about that edge. The word itself doesn't appear anywhere in the lyrics of her song, *East End Run*, which frames Montauk as the place you escape to when the world turns mad and you're ready to leave it all behind, but the idea is there—that, by design, this place is far from the center, out on the margins, where, as Atlas says, more may be demanded of you.

For one thing, living in Montauk is tougher than many places, which may be why the population of not-quite four thousand has shrunk consistently in the twenty-first century. Not just tougher to make a living because of the fishing regulations, but tougher in general. The weather is always a couple of degrees colder than in neighboring towns. The atmosphere is foggier. The shoreline craggier. Montauk is the first piece of land in the state to catch the sun's rays in the morning—and the first to lose the light in the afternoon. First light is the early wake-up call to leave the harbor's safety and go to work; last light means a long darkness.

Then there's that summer extravaganza when it's easy to believe there really are a quarter of a million people passing through the hamlet, when the pop-up shops and eateries and cycling gyms rise up like dandelions in the spring, and the parties and celebrities down the road in the Hamptons outdo last summer's parties and last year's celebrities—year after year. Until suddenly, at summer's end, all of that collapses. *Montauk* as an adjective stops meaning chic-and-upscale and goes back to meaning fishing-village-at-the-edge-of-the-earth—and if you have to ask what that feels like, you probably ought to go someplace else. The shift is profound. From sidewalks you cannot navigate because of the crowds and a clamor of noise that never dies, the town unwinds back to its not-quite four thousand residents, the Coast Guard station, the once-again-quiet Main Street where, on any given day, you can count on the fingers of one hand the number of fellow citizens you pass.

In fact, by November an almost-deadly quiet has taken hold, and all you've got is the people who live and work here year-round. They are the fishermen who keep going until January at least, then spend February and March with their boats drydocked so they can repair what needs repairing and be ready to go again in April.

A visitor will have trouble finding a hotel or motel to stay in during the Montauk winter. The few restaurants not shuttered "for the season" limit their hours or are only open weekends or only serve dinner—no lunch. No one starves: there's a modest-sized but well-stocked IGA supermarket that stays open late so you can do your shopping after work, while the 7-Eleven across the street never closes at all.

Days are calm and unruffled. The few businesses that keep going year-round because the work they do is year-round nevertheless close their doors against the chill, and the shops are closed because the customers are gone. So are many of the business owners and shopkeepers. They have headed south—and why not? They've probably worked seven days a week, ten hours a day for months. They need a break. They want a change of scenery. They go where they can find some ease and space, where you don't need a lot of clothes, where you don't have to worry about the heating bill.

George Watson closes up The Dock and heads south. Some of the fishermen do the same, Anthony Sosinski among them. On the first of January, when there's no more fishing to be done, he and his father move down to St. John, the smallest of the US Virgin Islands and an island of which two-thirds is National Park—unspoiled and bound by law to stay that way. They're there because John Sosinski always remembered a trip to St. John when he was in the Coast Guard, and in the days after his father's stroke, Anthony promised him that "if you get better, we'll go there every year." And so they do, staying through March in a house built into a hillside and sitting atop a thirty-thousand-gallon cistern. There Anthony dabbles in guiding paddleboard trips, captaining charters on a small sailboat he owns, running dive trips in the clear turquoise water, even trying his hand at silk-screening T-shirts. Regularly he takes his father to the beach, sets the older man's chair in ankle-deep surf, and together, father and son watch the butterflies, count the turtles, and keep their eyes peeled for possible dolphin sightings.

For Anthony this three-month experience of what he calls "straight-up paradise" is "my sanity spot." But despite that, he is always glad to get back to Montauk and the fisherman's life he has never been able to stay away from. At the end of the time away he feels more than ready to exchange the clear turquoise of Coral Bay for the gray chill of Montauk, lazy days on the beach for heading out with Johnny in the *Anna Mary*, away from safety to the dangerous work of commercial fishing. And while the rest of us shudder with relief that somebody else wants to do such work on our behalf, for these two men and others like them it is the only thing they want to do in life.

Montauk is the right place for fishermen. However the wider world may see it, Montauk sees itself as a fishing town. Fishermen *live* here, work here, play here—their lives can be contained here. Johnny's apartment, on the upper floor of a small, two-story building, is a stroll of five minutes' duration—if that—to the *Anna Mary*'s dock. A thirty-second stroll gets him to the beach. In effect, he can pretty much reach out and touch what's important to his life. Anthony lives a bit more inland in a low-slung house of traditional gray shingles with a garden out back where he and his father can grow everything from beans to zucchini, garlic to peppers to peas in summer. The house is a true classic: one of two hundred original Leisurama homes prefabricated and sold completely furnished by Macy's department store in 1963 and 1964. The subject of a documentary film* and of an exhibit at the 1964 World's Fair in New York, the Leisurama houses originally sold for around $12,000; today the sale price of a single one of them can run many, many times that. Like many of the houses, Anthony's has been tweaked and

---

* PBS, *Leisurama*, 2005.

reshaped inside until it perfectly suits his needs. It's his own, and from this comfortable perch he's only a bike ride away from the dock. That ride is the way he likes to start his day.

The days in Montauk move to a fisherman's rhythm. If you've ever lived or even stayed any amount of time in a fishing port, you know that these are early towns, in which the predawn vroom-vroom putt-putt of boats heading out of the harbor becomes part of the soundtrack of your dreams. Work days can start well before that—as early as two or three in the morning, with boats being loaded and engines churning to life. Then comes the afternoon packing out when the catch is unloaded, weighed, iced, and sold, and then come the drinks that follow around the bar as the crews unwind.

Fishermen set the tone of Montauk, and the fisherman's ethos is what counts there. "We're all a bunch of goofballs," says fisherman Phil Baigent, a friend of both Anthony and Johnny. And it's safe to say none of them are big on sentiment or letting your feelings hang out.

But feelings rode high that Wednesday morning, July 24, when cell phones started pinging with text messages and vibrating with voicemails: *Johnny Load has gone missing. He fell off the back of the Anna Mary, Little Anthony is looking for him, and the Coast Guard is on its way.*

Helen Battista is the quintessential friendly, engaging bartender, the kind of woman you immediately want to embrace and open up to. Ask any of the customers at Sammys, the popular dockside eatery and watering-hole where Helen works most days during the summer season, or ask any of her army of friends. Helen is a particularly close friend of Johnny Aldridge, whom she claims to have known "forever," and she got the message that he had gone overboard from her pal Ed in a text at 6:45 a.m. Ed was crewing for Breakaway charters that morning, and the trip was already well underway—until the radio distress call prompted the charter boat's captain, Richard Etzel, to cancel the trip and turn around. "We're going back in," he announced to his clients and crew. Ed tapped out the message to Helen right away: *Load fell off the boat last nite looking 4 him Fuck.*

Helen believes she actually got the message even earlier, at about 3:30 a.m., when she woke up—inexplicably and unaccountably—and could not fall asleep again. The text from Ed more than three hours later got her sitting bolt upright, feeling scared and alone. She didn't dare text or call anyone else: at 6:45 in the morning she knew she didn't want to spread rumors, and repeating the message only made it more true. Impelled by instinct, Helen dressed, leashed her dog, and walked down to the Montauk harbor just minutes away. Three fishermen and some other guys—Helen knew them all—were there, just hanging out, standing around. George Watson of The Dock was on the phone. "Whatever you have to do to get him back," Helen heard him growl into the phone.

"Is it true?" she asked the men standing there. "Have they found him?"

It was true, and at that hour of the morning Johnny was nowhere near being found.

The harbor became very busy very fast. Charter captains had already headed out with their paying customers aboard. Now, as the Breakaway's Richard Etzel had done, they were bringing their boats back, dropping off their customers—"Sorry, we won't be fishing today"—fueling up, and heading out again to look for Johnny. Guys hung around to make up crews for the boats going out.

Helen hung around too. The way she saw it, "everybody was going out—*everybody.*" And that meant that "they were going to get him." Pure and simple. She didn't let herself think beyond that. *They're just going out to get Load*, she kept telling herself. Until she had to be at work at eleven, this is where she would stay, watching the boats going out to get Load, secure in this space between The Dock and the jetty, between Watson's angry concern and the sound of boats on a quest.

Laurie Zapolski and Johnny Aldridge first crossed paths in 1994 and had been in and out of one another's lives ever since—a relationship Laurie herself characterizes as "on and off, to say the least." Yet the two of them have a long shared past. They attended the same middle school and high school, ran with the same crowd, came from a similar background, knew the same buzzwords. In a way they look like the proverbial opposites who should attract: Johnny dark and brooding and playing things close to the vest, Laurie a pretty blond with silky hair framing a cheerful, lively face and a dazzling smile. In reality both are strong-minded, sensible, appealingly grounded individuals. When they actually met, Johnny was in his early twenties, was nursing a broken heart—not uncommon for people in their early twenties—and was reluctant to the point of resistance to form a new commitment.

Laurie managed to cut through that, and there followed a decades-long on-again-off-again relationship. Each of them dated others, pointed their lives in different directions, and followed their separate pursuits. But they always somehow "gravitated toward one another"—the strength of their connection, whatever it was, pulling them together no matter how far apart they traveled from one another.

That summer of 2013 the relationship was off again. Johnny was dating a woman named Teresa, and Laurie was living miles from Montauk up-island, which is what East Enders call the suburbs to the west of Montauk, pursuing an advanced degree in education administration and working at the same time.

The call about Johnny's disappearance came from Tony Vincente, and it came to Laurie in her office early in the morning. Tony was an old friend and had been the guitarist in a band she used to sing with, but she had never heard anything like the way he sounded on the phone, and what he told her made her feel as if an intruder had entered her home and knocked her down. The news was too outlandish, unexpected, impossible. For a moment she felt rooted to her chair, unable to move.

Then something impelled her to search online and find a navigation chart for Montauk, as if by looking at the numbers, noting the ocean depth, and seeing the shapes of underwater topographic features she might be able to comprehend what had happened, where Johnny might be if he were still alive, what he might be going through, what he was thinking. She recalled that the last time they had been "on"—a particularly intense phase of their relationship—she had gone out on the *Anna Mary* with him and Anthony to watch them at work. Everything about their entire operation was so tightly controlled and worked so smoothly that the only possible cause she could think of for Johnny to have gone overboard was that something had hit him over the head.

Nothing about it made any sense. *I have to go to Montauk*, she decided. She said as much out loud to her coworkers as she left the office, went home, packed a bag, called to reserve a room, and drove—in what she admits was a quasi-hysterical and probably somewhat distracted state—to The End. She was aware that Johnny had a girlfriend right now, and although that meant she really couldn't seek out the Aldridge family but would instead have to keep to the shadows, she nevertheless texted Cathy to say she was on the spot if anything was needed.

The morning was wearing on. Laurie headed for The Dock.

Like drums in the jungle, the news of Johnny's disappearance spread through the fishing community, and one after another that day, professional fishermen and sport fishermen alike turned their work days into searches for John Aldridge. There were charter operators who tumbled their paying customers back onto the harbor dock, with apologies, so they could confine themselves to searching, while others, already at sea, shifted course and changed the content of the day's work. The concern stretched as far as the tugboat fleet in New York harbor, where former Montauk draggerman Tom "Boog" Powell, onetime captain of the *Wanderlust* on which

Johnny had worked, alerted tugs heading for the shipping lanes near Montauk to keep an eye out.

A party of shark hunters on Frank Braddick's forty-three-foot sport fisherman, *Hurry Up*, had just caught the mako they came for when Braddick heard Anthony's radio plea to any and all fishing vessels. That's when Braddick announced to his paying customers that they would now be trolling for tuna, although what he meant was that they would be trolling for John Aldridge—about thirty-five miles south of Montauk, looking to the west, the direction in which Braddick figured the drift would have taken him. The paying customers may never have known they were really fishing that day for a man lost at sea.

Paul Stern was another fishing professional out working that day, hired as a guide for a guy who wanted to catch a tuna—namely, music icon Jimmy Buffett. Summertime often finds the creator of "Margaritaville" and his yacht, the *Last Mango*, in Long Island waters, where he and Stern have fished together in the past. They were just getting underway that morning when Stern and *Last Mango* captain Vinnie La Sorsa heard the radio distress call about Johnny. *The Last Mango* is a fast boat, and Stern knew a fast boat could be useful. Would Buffett help? He told Stern, "Let's do whatever we have to do on this."

Dan Stavola had a fast boat too. Stavola is no fisherman. He's a contractor, but he is also a passionate Montauk guy who has been around boats and fishermen forever, and he knew Aldridge and Sosinski well. In fact, he and Anthony had once worked together, and neither of them is shy about saying

that the relationship had not been smooth. That didn't matter
now. When Stavola tuned into VHF, what mattered was the
bereft tone in Anthony's voice calling for help. *I have a boat
that flies*, he thought. *Let me see what I can do.*

The boat that flies was the *Cat in the Hat*, a fifty-foot sport-
fishing boat whose tower offered spotters a high, wide view of
the water, and whose engine could do more than thirty knots
an hour. Dan enlisted the help of Danny Lennox, Eddy Eurell,
and Donny Ball, whose own boat, the *Jen-Lissa*, is docked just
opposite the *Anna Mary*. The *Cat in the Hat* got underway a
little before 10 a.m., urged by Anthony to head east, down to
"the 500 line." They were there in less than an hour, and even
Anthony was momentarily surprised. "I forgot how fast you
go," he told Stavola over the radio. Dan captained the boat
while Lennox, Eurell, and Ball—two of them on the top tower,
one a single story up on the bridge—scanned the sea in all
directions. But hour after hour they saw nothing.

For the Viking Fleet's Steven Forsberg, Wednesday was to
have been a day off, one he had planned to spend with his
wife and five-year-old son fishing off one of the fleet's small
boats. Forsberg's grandfather had founded Viking, the charter fishing outfit both Anthony and Johnny had worked for
when they were in their teens and twenties. Forsberg's father
ran the business next, and now Steven runs it, along with
his older son, Steven Jr., and his nephew, Carl. But when he
heard the news about Johnny, Forsberg got hold of both of
them: "We gotta go," he told them. He readied the sixty-five-
footer instead of the small boat, and within forty-five minutes
of getting the message—he thinks somewhere around 10:00

a.m.—his crew of five, one of them a five-year-old boy, was heading out and around the Point.

Fast. Forsberg wanted to get there. He remembered from way back when Anthony's father used to work weekends for his father, and Anthony would come to Montauk as well, and the two of them would fish. Then Johnny started coming to Montauk too, and they became a trio—a crew of three boys fishing together whenever they could. So this was a friendship that went all the way back to childhood and all the way forward to right now.

Take a sixty-five foot, fully equipped commercial fishing vessel like Forsberg's or a fifty-foot sport-fishing yacht like Stavola's forty miles out to sea and run it "hour after hour," and you're burning fuel like it's going out of style—at a cost no one would want to think about. Neither Forsberg nor Stavola nor anyone else ever *did* think about it. The hell with cost. This was not a day for considering anything but Johnny Aldridge lost at sea, the fear in Anthony Sosinski's voice, the phone call the Aldridge family had received, and another family—the Montauk family—taking care of its own.

Steven Forsberg knew Johnny Aldridge well. He knew Aldridge was strong and in great shape. He knew the water was warm. He knew there was hope. He also had been on "many, many" search trips, and none of them had ever ended well. "You don't hear a lot of good news when somebody goes missing in the ocean," Forsberg says. But he also knew he wasn't going home until something was found.

Phil Baigent had been the one who notified Forsberg. A landlubber originally from Syracuse, Baigent first saw the

ocean when he was nine and the family moved to Stony
Brook. That's also when he got hooked on fishing. Nothing
stopped him after that—not even when his father didn't talk
to him for five years. "You can't make a fisherman," Phil says.
"You're just born one."

That morning the born fisherman hooked up with Al
Schaffer, the lobsterman who had been a mentor and partner
of Johnny, and they headed out together in Schaffer's boat,
aware that they were part of a growing armada heading out
to look for Johnny. It was odd, Baigent reflected as they left
the harbor, to see this closed, self-anointed, self-appointed,
exclusive fraternity of fishermen—normally a "bunch of goofballs," in his own phrase—suddenly turn deadly serious with
not a derisive bit of sarcasm in sight. He wondered to himself
whether Johnny had slipped and gone off the back of the boat
or if he had hit his head and then gone in. *Are we looking for
John or for a body?* Baigent wondered to himself.

There were things that cheered him: the weather was
warm, the water was warm, John was a bull. But the search
area was massive, and there was the memorial back on the
Point filled with the names of powerful, capable, smart fishermen who hadn't made it. Baigent desperately did not want
to see John Aldridge's name on the Lost At Sea Memorial, but
he couldn't get away from the feeling that the chances were
not good. *It's been a tough winter*, Baigent thought, *what with
the loss of Chubby Gray and a bunch of scary incidents. We
need something good to happen. We deserve it.*

Scallop fisherman Mike Skarimbas knows Johnny Aldridge as his closest friend. Skarimbas and his crew were well

offshore and hard at work that morning when, at "maybe 7:30 or 8:00," he heard Anthony's voice over the radio and a few disjointed words—"overboard," "missing"—and he knew his friend was in the water. "Right away," in his words, Skarimbas started steaming his vessel, the *New Species*, toward the *Anna Mary*'s gear, a location well known to him. Crew members Mario Negro and Sarah Broadwell climbed onto the roof and stayed there, eyes peeled.

Mike knew "without a doubt—a hundred percent—that Johnny was alive." The reason was simple. "Because I know *him*," says Skarimbas. The only question in his mind was whether they would find Johnny in time.

Skarimbas stationed himself in the wheelhouse. He was on a mission, and he was not going to move until the mission was accomplished. "All I could think of," he says, "was coming in and seeing Johnny's mother and father and telling them . . ." The sentence is never finished. Skarimbas breaks down—as he concedes, just as he broke down constantly that day.

"It was a horror for me," he says. "It was the worst day of my life. This is my best friend. I was an emotional wreck all day, staring at two computers and charts in the wheelhouse, thinking about drift and trying to figure out where he might be—where he could be." Up on the roof of the *New Species* Negro and Broadwell scanned the sea, every bit of exposed skin becoming more and more sunburned with every passing hour. They never said a word to one another, Broadwell admits. Both knew that the later the hour, the narrower the chance for good news, and neither of them was ready to say so out loud. "I kept imagining myself in the position Johnny was in," Broadwell says of her time scanning the sea from her high perch, "thinking about him alive and suffering out there. But after seven hours you had to figure we weren't going to find him."

Nancy Atlas had taken her kids somewhere or other and thinks it was sometime around 11:00 a.m. when she got the text from a friend: *Someone's fallen overboard from the Anna Mary.* The news jolted her. She is close with both *Anna Mary* captains, but she herself describes Anthony as her "surrogate brother," the guy you count on—always.

Nancy had a show at five o'clock that day. That was typical in the summer: open at five, close at sunset. She had to spend the day setting up the show—getting all the equipment in place and ready. She was also pregnant, so she wanted to rest from time to time. But the news about Johnny—and her fear for him—drove everything else out. Outwardly she made a point of staying optimistic, even if it felt a little like whistling as you pass a graveyard. She took to social media to call for "keeping everybody in our prayers" and tried hard to show only what she calls "positive energy." Everyone did the same without being told, for everybody knew without saying the words what the outcome could be. "We live in Montauk," says Atlas. "We know what happens."

There is, says Atlas, a kind of seasonal arc to the life of those who live in Montauk, an arc that visitors don't experience but that is second nature to the community of folks who make Montauk their home. In summer, she says, "everyone is disconnected." That is the working season, the revenue-generating season, the time of feeding the extravaganza, when "fishermen are fishing, waitresses are serving, singers are singing. In summer your head is down and you are in work mode." It is a whole different ballgame from October or March, when the tourists are gone, the traffic is gone, the summer people are gone, and "everyone is connected."

But on that July day, at the height of "work mode," at the peak of the time when heads are down, "everything stopped suddenly," says Atlas. "The summer thing evaporated, and the communal web descended."

"Communal web" is the kind of phrase Nancy Atlas comes up with all the time, which is probably why she is a songwriter and musician. But that day the communal web seemed palpable, muting even the tourists settling in for lobster and crab lunches, slowing the normally frantic pace of buying and selling, of arriving and leaving. Summer's head-down mode had turned wintry, and while the Montauk community seemed suddenly connected in a winter way, there was a chill over the place.

Chapter 9

To the West-End Buoy

Approximately 10:00 a.m.

All night I had been clinging to this idea of finding a buoy. Now I had totally exhausted myself trying to get to one, only to realize that the buoy I am after is out of my reach. What now? What do I do? The battle starts up in my head, and it is almost as exhausting as the swim. Do I keep fighting to get to this unreachable goal? Or do I find another way? What other way? What freaking other way is there? And what about the energy wasted—just wasted—trying to get to this unreachable buoy. The very idea of the waste—of energy, time, everything—freaks me out. *You screwed up,* I tell myself. *How are you going to get out of it? Or is this just going to be the end of your life?*

But these are the thoughts that can kill, and I have to send them packing. What is strange is that I know how to do this.

I've learned that I have the power to swipe these kinds of thoughts off the screen of my brain. It's that or die. Let the thoughts in, and they will overtake me and I will be headed down the hole to the end of my life. And that is impossible; I cannot let that happen.

I close my eyes for a second. I picture the thoughts that can take me to my death, and I shake them out of my head. I just do.

When I open my eyes, there it is. There is a buoy.

What I glimpse first is a flutter of orange. Orange is the color of the flag on Pete's west-end gear. Then I ride the crest of another swell, look again lower down, and see the red polyball. Red buoy, orange flag: that confirms it. This is Pete Spong's west-end buoy. But it is very, very far away. I have no real idea of the distance, but I tell myself it is three or four hundred yards away. What is that? How far is that? On land it is three or four football fields. That's a walk around the block on dry land. That's what? Like a quarter of a mile? half a mile? Not even. It is nothing. *Think about getting there*, I tell myself. *Think about that instead of about dying.*

But getting there is hard work. And it is painfully slow. Ride up on the crest, see the buoy, down into the trough, see nothing but ocean. Swim, swim, rest. Swim, swim, rest. Switch hands, then swim again. Keep going. Endure.

I am ingesting a lot of water. The sea pours into my mouth when I breathe, and I know that at some point too much of it could swamp the flap over my windpipe and shut my airway. But if I close my mouth, the water just goes up my nose. That is just as bad, and the salt stings. *Plug your nose*, I think. *Plug it.* I

The *Anna Mary* in her slip
at the Town Dock, Montauk.
Note the open stern.

Johnny Aldridge in the Vermont
woods, late autumn, 1990.

Anthony Sosinski, Sheepshead Bay, Islip, New York,
eight years old, same size as the fish.

Johnny with a just-caught lobster.

Anthony and Johnny aboard the *Anna Mary*, preparing for a trip out, this time with a gate on the stern.

Pete Spong's deckhand examining the knot Johnny tied and the two polyballs he tied together when he finally came to rest.

Mike Migliaccio, preparing to crew for a trip on the *Anna Mary*.

Johnny being lifted into the MH-60, hanging on for dear life.
Courtesy of Coast Guard rescue mission fisherman PO1 Robert Simpson

USCG rescue swimmer Bob Hovey and the man he rescued aboard the MH-60, July 24, 2013.
Courtesy of AST3 Robert Hovey

Cathy's broadcast text, transmitted from the Coast Guard's Station Montauk, when she knew her brother was alive...

Anthony getting ready to fillet the tuna caught on the way home, July 24, 2013. *Courtesy Sheila Rooney*

Home. Johnny and his nephew, Jake Patterson, in front of the Aldridge house in Oakdale, answering questions from the press. *Courtesy of Kevin Quinn*

Johnny, his sister, Cathy Patterson, and brother, Anthony Aldridge, at the Blessing of the Fleet.

From left to right, Anthony and his daughters Emma and Melanie.

Anthony pulls up a highflyer to find Johnny's tag: "Load Lives."

Montauk's own George Watson,
proprietor of the legendary
watering-hole and restaurant,
The Dock.

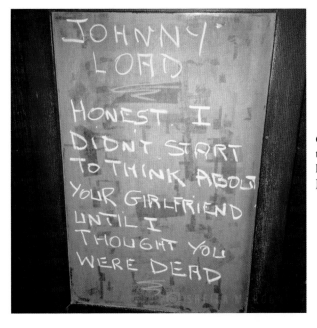

George Watson's message on
the chalk board at The Dock,
his way of announcing that
Johnny had made it.

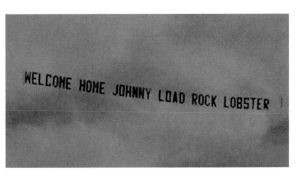

The message that was flown
above the Oakdale barge party to
celebrate Johnny's rescue.

The first occurrence of the annual Blessing of the Fleet the year after Johnny's rescue.

Johnny Aldridge, suitably attired, at the Oakdale barge party celebrating his rescue.

Johnny's first fishing trip after his rescue, back aboard the *Anna Mary*, with a benign ocean, beautiful sunset, and lobsters for company.

consider stopping, cutting up one of my socks, using the pieces to plug my nose. But I don't want to stop. I want to get there.

Then I think of another use for the socks. I realize I need more pull with the hand I am using to scoop the water backward in my one-armed half-crawl half-sidestroke. I grab a sock off my foot and put the wet fabric over my hand like a mitten. This gives me webbing so I can catch more water when I pull.

At the next crest I look up, and there's Pete. Himself. His boat, the *Brooke C*, is up ahead. I can see him in the distance going along the line of his gear. He's on the deck railing, looking down, looking at the water, maybe checking his gear, maybe looking for me. I stop swimming and start screaming, yelling, waving my gloved hand in the air. Nothing. He can't see me; he can't hear me. The waves are obscuring his sight lines as well as mine, even though he is not far from me, not far at all. I am up and down, up and down, eyes focused, when I can see anything at all, on getting to the west-end buoy. And in a matter of seconds he is gone. I freak out. Nothing, nothing, nothing good is happening.

Then I say to myself, *All right, try to stay positive. Keep going. You have to keep going.*

I swim. *Think about getting there*, I tell myself. I feel a twinge of pain in my leg—a spasm. The first hint of a charley horse. *Forget about that*, I tell myself. *Nothing is going to stop me. No physical pain is going to dictate the outcome of this swim. No way. I give in to pain, and I die. It's that simple.*

I put the pain away, stash it right next to the doubts about survival I have shaken out of the garbage bin of my brain. I know how to do that too, how to put away pain or discomfort. All fishermen do. We have to know. You stand in smelly fish slime amid tangled miles of rope on a rocking-and-rolling boat for fifteen hours at a stretch, wearing big, sweaty rubber gloves and hauling metal traps up from the ocean floor, emptying them, measuring and banding the catch, then re-setting the traps with bait and lowering them again: that's the work of the job. There's no alternative, so you don't even think about pain or discomfort. You do this work when it's cold and clammy and sleeting so hard you can barely see what you're doing, and you do it under a broiling sun when you're dripping rivers of sweat so hard you can barely see what you're doing. And on the *Anna Mary*, when we've finished with one trawl and are heading for the next, we're trolling for tuna or mahi-mahi, which means a whole different set of equipment to set up and monitor, plus keeping pressure on multiple lines at once. And of course we also have to operate the boat, watch the weather, maintain our cooling tanks. So you're tired, you're sore, something aches, something stings, it's too hot, it's too cold—thank you for sharing, but this is the job. Get back to work.

Same with construction. Same work ethic. Heat, rain, fly-ing hammers, falling planks, murderous power tools, scream-ing clients—all of it and more. This is the job we do, and there is no alternative but to get it done.

Now my job is to be in the water, swimming with one arm and switching from flutter kick to frog kick and back again, and there is Pete's west-end buoy up ahead, and that is all that counts. Only the need to get to the west-end buoy counts.

Which means that both physically and mentally I have to stay inside that need to keep swimming. Neither my body nor my brain can be anywhere else. This is the job. There is no other job. So I keep going.

But the buoy is still far away, and it is such slow going. I come up on a crest, and there's the *Anna Mary*. She is close. How did I miss her this close? She is traveling north on the same trackline we came south along, and there is Mike up on the roof, looking for me. Again I scream and wave, and again I am neither heard nor seen. Yet oddly it brings my mood up a bit to see my boat, and I can see the dot of that helicopter overhead as well. There is definitely a search on; they are working a pattern searching for me. *Stay positive*, I tell myself again and again. *Stay positive. They're looking for me. I'm not so lost as all that, not so isolated as before.*

Still, the certainty that they are searching for me makes my swim ever more urgent. Searching isn't finding—it's only looking. If I am to be rescued, I need to be visible, and to be visible, I need to get to the buoy. I keep going. Swim, swim, rest. Swim, swim, rest. I am getting closer. Closer. Maybe two hours after I started, I arrive.

I get a hand on the bright red buoy, then grasp the rope tethering it to the ocean floor. I can stop propelling myself. For the first time since I fell into the water—how long ago? six hours? seven hours? more?—I am holding onto something fixed. For the first time something other than my own effort is keeping me steady.

Chapter 10

Command and Control

10:00 a.m.

They say that twenty-three boats headed out from Montauk that day—a volunteer armada comprising commercial and sport vessels of various sizes and shapes, all bent on a single objective. Yet at the time, for mission coordinator Jonathan Theel in the command center in New Haven, the whole idea of the volunteers chomping at the bit to get into action presented something of a quandary.

Years of both training and experience in SAR management had taught Theel that coordinating a search-and-rescue mission consisted of at least two tasks: one was coordinating the search and rescue; the other was managing the event. Managing the event meant many things, all of them important, none of them directly integral to the task of planning a search and directing assets to execute it.

Managing the event meant, for example, staying in contact with the family, which Theel was trying to do—or have someone do—as close to once an hour as possible.* It meant dealing with the community, which, fortunately for Theel, was today a job for Dennis Heard at Montauk Station. Public or press relations are always an issue, but again, in this case the issue affected Montauk Station more than the New Haven command center. And then there were the Good Samaritan volunteers, the people who offer every variety of assistance when someone is in trouble or in need of aid.

Volunteers act out of good will, not out of self-interest. They tend to be unreserved in the generosity with which they expend their energy, their intelligence, their own resources. But when you are managing a SAR, it is also essential to keep in mind that these volunteers are not under your control, they do not answer to you, and yet you may be assuming liability for anything and everything they do.

That is why over the years Theel believed he had learned two truths about making use of volunteer assistance: one truth holds that you make use of volunteers at your peril. The equal but opposite truth holds that you fail to make use of volunteers at your peril. The fishing vessels coming out en masse to search for John Aldridge could certainly add value to a search. Their captains and crews knew the territory far better than the Coast Guard officers in their lifeboats and response boats—good seamen all, but not intimately familiar

---

* John and Adeline Aldridge remember receiving those hourly calls—and remain grateful for them.

with the fishing grounds off Long Island, waters where, as the Coast Guard knew, there are eddies and swirls that computer models simply cannot and do not cover. The volunteers also knew one another and could communicate quickly across their fishermen's network. And they knew John Aldridge and Anthony Sosinski.

Theel was particularly aware that telling a fisherman he or she cannot do something is a difficult proposition. He also admits that in their shoes he would be doing exactly what all of Montauk's fishing vessel and charter boat captains were doing. The fraternity of "all of us that live on the sea," Theel says, "accepts absolutely the unwritten rule that you help someone in distress. Period."

But he also saw how difficult the arrival of twenty-three volunteer fishing vessels could be when it came to coordinating an effort, and he worried especially about the potential impact on the SAROPS planning process of inputting data from twenty-three separate navigational positions. What he finally settled on seemed the perfect way to make use of the volunteers' knowledge and their multiple additional eyeballs while keeping them safe, helping free the Coast Guard to do what it does best, and not blowing up the computer.

He put Anthony Sosinski in charge of the volunteer fleet. Anthony had been communicating with the fishing vessels from the outset, he was a colleague and friend of the captains of these vessels, and, once again, he and they spoke a common language. The plan was for Anthony to assign each of the volunteer fishing vessels its own search site in the greater grid of Aldridge's probable location. He would task each participating vessel to run a slot due north and south, plotting each slot at a distance of a half mile from the next vessel's slot. In that way the fishing boats would build a fence that would bound a substantial portion of the search area and cover the waters within the fence from end to end and from side to side. And they would do all of this in their own language—speaking in Loran terms and in Long Island Sound fishing vernacular.

They did exactly that—twenty-three Montauk commercial fishing and/or charter vessels under the command of Anthony Sosinski. In addition to the other benefits these actions produced, Anthony would later claim that managing the volunteer fleet is what kept him sane through the day.

Shirtless, wearing only his shorts, he stationed himself against the starboard railing of the *Anna Mary*, a vantage from which he could scan the ocean even as he operated the radio microphone, stretched on its cord from the radio base in the wheelhouse. He would regularly stick his head back into the wheelhouse to check coordinates on the Loran, also positioned in the wheelhouse a mere five feet away, as he spoke into the mic and alternately held it to his ear to hear.

Coordinating the fleet essentially meant juggling communications channels—and knowing the relevant ocean real estate like the back of your hand. Sosinski's first move had been to broadcast on Channel 16 to all vessels involved in the civilian search to switch to Channel 1—it was the channel Montauk fishermen tended to use to communicate with one another when they were at sea, and it seemed the appropriate place. He continued to use Channel 16 to connect to the Coast Guard command center, while Channel 22 was his line to the Coast Guard helicopter, the eye in the sky in the search for Johnny. He was operating the radio in the Scan position, so he would frequently be talking to one vessel on Channel 1 when another would hail him—"Hey, Anthony, the Coast Guard wants to talk to you on Sixteen"—and he would switch over, then switch back to 1 to update the volunteer vessels, then over to 22 to get the position of the MH-60 copter, and so it went.

He assigned slots in the grid based on where the volunteer vessel was when it called in its longitude and latitude and on his own assessment of where Johnny might have drifted to at this point. In a sense he was moving the fleet with the drift. For example, when he heard from a friend on the fifty-eight-foot *Bookie*, which was tile fishing fifty miles to his southeast, he assigned that vessel to the easternmost slot in the grid because it would be arriving at the slot from the east. He also made educated guesses: "Steam three miles east," he might order a boat, "then look north and south," just trying to anticipate where the drift might have taken his partner and friend of a lifetime while hoping—but not knowing—that he was safe on a buoy somewhere in this great big ocean.

That was Anthony's post, and he never left it.

Neither did the very parched Mike Migliaccio leave *his* post, except for an occasional jump down to the deck to grab another bottle of water. Mike "lived on the roof" of the boat, in Anthony's phrase, "smoking Marlboro Reds like they were free." The two men had known one another since Mike's brother, a chef by trade, had died in a fire in an apartment Anthony had once lived in. He and Anthony met when Mike came to Montauk to see where his brother had died. In time Migliaccio, a skilled marine mechanic, decided to make Montauk his home and to go back to sea with the fishing fleet. That day the Charles Bronson lookalike had only his hat for protection against the sun as he stood, wearing the blue jeans and T-shirt that were his standard uniform, beside the mast among the huge lights and crisscrossing ropes. A pair of binoculars was locked onto his eyes; by day's end the glasses had stenciled two large white patches on a face otherwise sunburned to the point of lobster redness.

This was the first "overboard incident" Mike had ever been associated with, and they were looking for a friend. *If anybody can make it, Johnny will*, he told himself. But as the hours clicked on, holding that thought grew more and more difficult, and Mike himself grew increasingly anxious.

At four hours he started thinking about sharks. At six hours he began to worry about hypothermia. Still, adrenaline and affection and worry kept him fastened to his post. Regularly he shouted encouragement from beyond the grave down to Anthony: "My brother tells me it will be all right. Keep looking." Keeping on looking was what he did nonstop. "I checked every wave for 360 degrees around me, over and over," Migliaccio says. "I tried to follow where the tide was going and how the wind was blowing. I searched all over. I saw a lot of boats"—the volunteer armada filling the slots of the grid—"but it just wasn't happening."

Meanwhile the mission team in New Haven turned its attention to consideration of the two standard options for extending the Aldridge search after dark—either pull assets back and restart the search "hard" in the morning, or search all night. They committed the mission to search all night if needed, certain that the assets currently involved in the search plus additional resources in reserve were more than sufficient. Those additional reserves included the cutters *Tiger Shark* and *Sailfish*, due to arrive at the search zone later, which Theel would assign to take over the command and control of the fleet overnight.*

But it wasn't nighttime yet. The sun was still bright, there was plenty of daylight left, and the volunteer fleet was very much out there, each vessel following the slot in the ocean Anthony had assigned, back and forth, up and down in a part of the grid where they would not be duplicating any other boat's search—lots more eyeballs trained on the sea looking for Johnny Aldridge.

What is it like to keep staring at the sea, looking for a person in the water? Boatswain's Mate Rich Standridge, a Coastie who was *not* involved in the Aldridge SAR, says that "from an operator's standpoint, I can tell you it is so hard to see anything. I always thought before I came into the service: *It's bright orange or red or yellow on a blue ocean. It ought to be easy.* But it really is like looking for a needle in a haystack." A lot of volunteer crew members spent a lot of time in the crow's nests of a lot of boats that day, "getting very

---

* As it turned out, neither cutter ever got to the search zone—the *Sailfish* was delayed for refueling while the *Tiger Shark* had an antenna problem and had to head back to port. Thankfully neither cutter was needed.

sunburned," as veteran fisherman Chuck Weimer observed, as they searched for that needle.

Steve Forsberg thinks his was about the eleventh boat to get his assignment. Steven Jr. was driving the boat; Carl and Forsberg took the highest point on the wheelhouse. He told his younger son, "Look for anything," but even as he said it, he knew how fruitless an exercise that was likely to be. Scanning the moving ocean for someone's head was like looking for a particular grain among all the grains of sand on the beach.

Cathy Patterson and her sister-in-law, Jillian, arrived at Station Montauk at the end of Star Island Road at around 10:30. Tommy's partner, Rob Howard, their "escort" from the deputy sheriff's office, rang the bell at the gate and announced who they were, and they were buzzed in. Dennis Heard, the acting officer in charge, was alerted to their presence and came forward to greet them.

The main building of the Montauk Station is big and rather stately. White with a red-tiled roof, it is two stories high under the ample roof, while the roof itself holds garret rooms and a lookout tower at its peak. Spacious though the building appears, it consists mostly of offices, conference rooms, a cafeteria and similar utilities, and operational spaces where USCG functions are carried out. No particular provision has been made for visitors like Cathy and Jillian. Heard was gracious and sympathetic and ushered the women into the building's communications suite, where Cathy remembers seeing half a dozen people studiously monitoring an array of large computer screens. Heard opened a large file cabinet and pulled a navigational chart out of the drawer. "Here is where the *Anna Mary* is now," he said, pointing with his finger. He showed her the coordinates where they thought Johnny might have gone overboard and outlined the probable search area.

Cathy remembers thinking something was "off" when they showed her the coordinates for the top of the search area—an instinct telling her that her brother would have been farther out, closer to his fishing area. But the Coast Guard had the experts, had all this equipment, had all these search capabilities Dennis Heard was now explaining to her—patrol boats, response boats, helicopters, jets, cutters, SAROPS. The service's competence was right there in the name, SAROPS: Search and Rescue Optimal Planning System—the latest and best tool for search and rescue the Coast Guard had, which pretty much made it the latest and best tool for search and rescue anywhere in the world. SAROPS could ingest more and more data streaming in from the boats out there and from the planes overhead, plus data from anywhere in the world about tides and currents and winds, and the system would simulate various scenarios, measure probabilities, spit out fresh coordinates and new plans. Surely they knew best.

Heard needed to get back to work, and he summoned two of the storekeepers to stay with Cathy and Jillian. Coast Guard storekeepers are nonoperational staff who handle supply, storage, logistics, and office functions. Two of the storekeepers at Montauk Station at the time were women, and Heard thought their company—if Cathy and Jillian needed company—would be a good idea. The storekeepers showed Cathy and Jillian the mess deck and the porch, and it was there, outside, where Cathy and Jillian settled in to wait and watch, their eyes trained straight out to sea.

The station began to fill with people. Teresa, the woman Johnny was dating at the time, showed up, as did other friends. And local law enforcement officials began descending on the station. The Suffolk County sheriff's office was already there, having provided the escort, but it belonged there for another reason as well. As befits a coastal county, the office has its own marine patrol section and is part of what is called the East End Marine Task Force, which comprises eighteen policing agencies from the five East End towns and their multiple villages and hamlets as well as from the State Park Police and the state Department of Environmental Conservation. The alert for Johnny had activated just about all of them, and the heads of the various departments were now converging on the station. This was right, proper, and essential: with two of Montauk Station's vessels out on the search and a third ready to relieve one of them, any other marine emergency would have to be met by vessels from the fleet represented by the Task Force.

As Dennis Heard was finding out, however, a lot of the local law enforcement officials had a lot of questions. Some of the questions were requests for information updates, which Dennis answered as best he could, and some were somewhat insistent questions about what the Coast Guard was doing. Heard tried to answer everyone patiently—"I knew they wanted to help out," he says—but he feared that repeating the same story time and again to different individuals and assuring local officials, who "wanted to launch every boat around," that it wasn't yet time to do so was taking him away from his primary responsibility. *Please*, he wanted to say, *we may indeed need your boats in due course, but it is not the right move at this time, so please just step back and let us do our jobs . . .*

Tommy Patterson arrived at about noon. His parents had come to the house and picked up their grandson Jake, and Tommy had put on his uniform and gone on duty. He took the sheriff's car and drove, as assigned, to Montauk Coast Guard Station. He joined Cathy and Jillian and other friends all doing the same thing—waiting.

Text messages flew into Cathy's phone. The gist of all of them was the same: *Hang in there.* She was not about to do anything else.

She remembered when Chubby Gray had been lost the previous December. That was an eternity ago, yet right now the loss felt fresh and opened a deep, dark, cold hole in her heart. Chubby had been "one of the boys," a friend of Johnny and Anthony, a young guy taking his cue from the veterans like her brother and his partner. What made the loss even worse were all the question marks: What had happened? What could have made that boat, a twin of the *Anna Mary*, and the two experienced seamen aboard her simply disappear? Cathy remembered how shaken Johnny was at the time, and how he said to her: "I just want you to know that if something like that ever happens to me, I will do everything I can to survive and come back to you." Whatever the outcome, she would know that he had fought every minute with all his strength to stay alive. She was counting on that now.

She needed to count on something as she stayed in touch with the family back in Oakdale. Her father was in the process of convincing himself that his oldest son was dead. Or maybe he had already done so. Either way, she feared he was coming unglued. Clinging to Johnny's promise that he would not stop trying, she would not believe her brother was gone, refused even to admit the idea into her head. "I *never* thought he was dead," she remembers emphatically, even if only because such a thing was unthinkable. But all around her in the station, it seemed, she could see in people's faces the probability that Johnny was gone. "What are the odds?" Tommy had asked a group of Coasties staring at a chart. They gave no answer, just turned their heads away. After that, Cathy remembers, "I didn't want to look at Tommy. He had the look of someone thinking Johnny was gone," and she couldn't bear to see it.

Heard estimates there were more than forty "outside" people in the station. They moved mostly between the mess deck and the front porch, and he bounced from one to the other, offering information updates. He could see what they were going through, and he was conscious of trying to keep his own emotions in check. *Just let them know what we absolutely know,* he said to himself, *even if it's not much and even though it's the same thing I told them an hour ago.*

With a staff of six, he was also monitoring the staging of the other marine patrols, those that would cover for the offshore Coast Guard vessels if needed. He relayed the permission from the New Haven command center for the small response boat captained by Jason Walter to go out as far as twenty miles offshore—an exception allowed because of the life-and-death situation and because the water was calm enough. He was in regular communication with the command center and was tuned in to the communications among the boats of the growing volunteer fleet. In fact, when New Haven experienced a communications glitch, Montauk Station had to fill them in on where the volunteer fleet was. There were instructions on what Dennis should tell the family—and what he should not tell the family—and when a team of specialists trained in dealing with next of kin might be assembled and deployed.

As if that weren't enough, he had been told that there was a retirement party being held that morning up at the lighthouse for an E-10, a master chief petty officer—the senior enlisted rank in the Coast Guard—and the station should expect a visit. Fortunately the E-10 showed up early in the day and, as a veteran of many operations, understood exactly what the staff were up against and graciously took his leave. Only much later would Heard appreciate the irony of being asked to host a retiree on such a day.

Dennis Heard is an easygoing, mild-mannered man with a calming presence. But behind that, as he bounced from task to task, from need to need, from one constituency to the other, he admits that having the family on site was "stressful." He wanted to be sure they were getting the information they needed; he also wanted to be sure they weren't hearing things that weren't helpful. And he was grateful for the storekeepers, who had mastered a level of ease in talking to family members that he could only envy.

Machinery Technician Second Class Brian Giunta felt a different kind of stress from the presence of the Aldridge family members. Although relieved that he did not have to deal directly with the sister of the missing man as Dennis Heard did, the fact that family members were right there at the station intensified the burden of responsibility he was there to undertake. Giunta was assigned that day to serve as engineer on the *second* forty-seven-foot lifeboat, the one due to go out after the first one returned from the search. He was in waiting mode that morning—in readiness—and for him the assignment was personal. He knew of the two lobstermen; he remembered Sosinski—Little Anthony, as he called him—as the guy who rode a unicycle in the local Saint Patrick's Day parade, a natural clown. And to him, "Johnny's family being here brought a whole other element" to his assignment.

In his years of search-and-rescue work Giunta, in his own words, "pulled a lot of bodies out of the water." When his crew was assembled the morning of July 24, 2013, primed to relieve the 47 on its return from the search, "we looked at each other, and we knew we all had the worst-case scenario in mind."

"It's inevitable," Giunta goes on. "You're dealing with the North Atlantic Ocean—the sea is in control at all times." But the reality of family members gathered there, of Aldridge's sister standing on the porch looking out to sea, "hit home," Giunta says. He realized with dramatic immediacy that he—and his crew and their training and the forty-seven-foot patrol boat they were assigned to—were, in the eyes of the family, a lifeline, their sole hope of getting Johnny Aldridge back home alive. That realization added to the weight of responsibility he knew was on them all, but it also made Giunta feel ever more acutely that he was ready to take on the responsibility.

Cathy felt heartened when she was told that a fleet of local fishing vessels had gone out from Montauk to aid in the search, all coordinated into an organized grid by Anthony. Dennis Heard called the mobilization an "exceptional" response and said the local fleet was freeing the Coast Guard to concentrate its own resources. Cathy felt good hearing that, and the place was bustling with activity—Coasties coming and going, phones buzzing and chirping, computer screens alive with shifting graphics.

It was just a few minutes before 1:00 p.m. when Cathy became aware of "something" happening. She felt a shift in the vibe, something different about the way the department heads comported themselves and looked at one another. In normal circumstances Cathy Patterson's mind is diamond-sharp; in the present circumstances her sensors were on overdrive, and what she was sensing caused her stomach to drop. *What was going on? Something had happened, but what? Were they slowing down the search? Giving up? Why had things at the station gone off track? Things had to get back on track.* The "business mode" that is so natural to Cathy kicked in. Raising her voice and effectively calling everyone in the station to order, Cathy Patterson made a speech.

"This is no ordinary fisherman," she said, her voice both taut with worry and rigid with authority. "This is my brother. Don't end this search. Promise me. Promise you will not give up."

There was no question of giving up. Two hours beforehand the order had gone out to continue searching through the night and into the morning. And although boats might come back to the station to resupply and refuel, and although crews might hit their sustainability limit and have to be replaced by other crews, it takes an order from the district level—above the sector command—to call off a search, and even then, as Jason Walter says, "it doesn't happen fast."

Not long thereafter Walter himself returned to the station from the search. The crew of four had been out for some six hours in the small response boat, had been cleared to search beyond its normal range, and, given the boat's speed, had been able to search over a relatively sizeable area. But there was no sign of Johnny Aldridge when the crew, tired and a bit dejected, was ordered to head back to the station.

As they turned into the inlet they were stunned to see "fifty or more people," in Walter's words, lining the beach, wait-ing and watching. The crowd surged forward. "Did you find him?" people shouted. "Have you got Johnny?"

Glumly, they shook their heads.

What Cathy didn't know about that shift in the air pressure at a few minutes before 1:00 p.m.—what she would learn only much later—was that back in the command center in New Haven, at 12:45 p.m., SAROPS had crashed.

Jason Rodocker attributes the crash to data overload. The system was simply swamped by all the added information coming in from the volunteer fleet—it was too big a bite to swallow. Rodocker is a slender man, yet the fingertips of his hands seem particularly well padded—maybe the result of so much time spent at keyboards, maybe an added reason he is so good at the work. Either way, Jason recognized the crash as something that sometimes just happens with computers—a reality of his job. "I have to keep rolling till somebody relieves me," he says, the fingertips flying over the keys as he works. That wasn't going to happen for a while, so Rodocker rebooted, started over, and kept going.

But around him in the command center in New Haven and in the communications suite at Montauk Station, the suddenly stilled computer screen seemed eerie, and the staff felt the dip in the atmosphere. Six-plus hours after notification, in what was turning into a prolonged case, to lose your most powerful technical tool was a blow. Until the multicolored particles could again be seen clustering on a monitor, everyone felt that where finding Johnny Aldridge was concerned, they were now as good as flying blind.

Chapter 11

The Landward Watch

Noon

The Aldridge house in Oakdale was bursting at the seams, filled with people who knew only that they wanted to be present to support John and Addie, to embrace Anthony, who seemed almost broken by despair, to encircle the family in a chain of love that would withstand whatever was going to happen in the hours ahead.

But they were also there for their own sakes. Partly they felt a need to be with other people who knew Johnny. And partly they were there because today was fast becoming what Tony Vincente called "one of the worst days of my life." And when you are having one of the worst days of your life, who can bear to be alone?

Those who gathered there had not accepted that Johnny was gone. With all his might, Tony didn't want to believe it. Steve D'Amico didn't believe it at all, not for a second. "I didn't have the feeling that he was gone," D'Amico recalls. "I knew the water was warm and that Johnny would know what to do. I hoped he was doing it."

D'Amico had reason to believe in the power of Johnny Aldridge's strong mind, a mind powerful enough to show him whatever he had to do to stay alive. He remembered an incident from when they were young guys hanging out together, a bit of fun gone wrong that D'Amico believed summed up the man Johnny Aldridge became. The two were in their late teens, young men strutting their stuff, and what better or at least noisier way to do it than on dirt bikes? Steve and Johnny each owned one, and they liked to take them into the woods to run them up and down a big mound of soil, gravel, and debris left behind by a construction crew. The name of the game was to see how high they could jump the bikes, and there was always a bit of bravado to it, not to mention a bit of competitiveness.

Steve took his run and went pretty high, and as he landed he looked back and saw Johnny jumping "way high" and at a pretty fast clip. In fact, Johnny was going so fast and flying so high that his feet shot off the bike pegs at the very top of the jump. He lost control, and when he finally crash landed, in addition to his many cuts, scratches, and bruises, the left peg scraped his shin, cutting it open to the bone. The two boys immediately recognized the injury as one that obviously needed attention, which meant getting him to a hospital fast, and because his bike was out of commission—temporarily anyway—Steve took him there on his own, positioning Johnny on the back of the bike as best he could and driving through the city streets to the nearest emergency room.

This was illegal, as dirt bikes are not permitted on town streets, but no cop stopped them, and they made it to the hospital without further disasters. Before he gave himself over to the emergency room staff, however, Johnny begged Steve to hide his crashed dirt bike at the D'Amico house. Although Johnny thought he could shrug off his own bruises as not too bad, he was afraid that if his father saw the mauled bike, he would recognize how serious the crash had been and would try to get rid of it. And as Johnny conceded, "it wasn't the bike's fault"—it was his for trying to outdo Steve. He was ready to pay for that sin in pain he would try to obscure, but he did not want to lose the bike.

Steve thought of that contest now, in the Aldridge living room. He thought about a guy who was always trying to go higher, a guy who took his lumps when he had to and didn't cry about it, a guy whose mind was consistently dealing with solutions to the problem and with endings that made sense. He figured that guy had to be alive out there on the water and that he was working through it in some way or other.

But whatever you thought or believed or conjectured or hoped, the not knowing was awful: the minutes—then the hours—dragging by without any word at all, the silence instead of answers, and no certainty about when the answers might come. So there were faces moist with tears. There were soft voices. And there were supportive words, reassurance, encouragement. "Don't worry," Tony Vincente insisted to Addie and John senior and to everyone else. "Johnny is alive. He is sitting on a buoy waiting, and soon he's going to surf his way back. He's alive." The more obdurately you believed it, the worse the waiting seemed.

Addie Aldridge believed absolutely. "He was a survivor from birth," says his mother of Johnny Aldridge. Born with pneumonia, he was not expected to live through the first seventy-two hours of life, even after being transported to a hospital that boasted advanced neonatal care facilities. But Addie didn't believe the medical prognosis and never shed a tear. "I just assumed he would be fine," she says. "Nothing is going to happen to him, and he's going to be fine." That is what she told herself as a young, first-time mother, and back then it all worked out exactly that way. "He *was* fine," she says. "He made it. That's what I mean that he was a survivor from birth. I didn't see him till he was five days old, but I knew he would be fine."

Forty-five years later she held fast to the same confident knowledge. Surrounded by friends and family who were there to keep watch with her, the same assumption took hold. "I didn't have that feeling in my heart that he wasn't with us anymore," she says. "I felt that he was alive and they would find him." Her Johnny would be fine again, just as when he was an infant—she knew it.

But at the moment the waiting had to be endured, and no one could even guess how long that would last.

How long could it last? the people there wondered to themselves—not aloud, not within earshot of John or Addie or Anthony. *How many hours could anyone survive in the ocean*

*without a life jacket, without anything, even in the summer?
And how would the ordeal end? Would they find a body? An
article of clothing? His boots floating on the waves? Would the
Coast Guard just call off the search?* When they search and
search and find nothing, the next thing you hear is that they
have ended the search. And there's nothing—no body to bury,
no trace, no remnant, absolutely nothing.

The phone rang frequently, and at each ring people held
their breath. Family members and friends would try to field
and screen the calls. If it was the Coast Guard—an officer
phoning them every hour or so, almost religiously—John Aldridge was sure they were calling to say they had spotted a
body. If it wasn't the Coast Guard, then it was yet another
friend or neighbor asking the same questions they were asking themselves or expressing the same concern everyone
there felt. How many times, after all, could John senior or
Addie be expected to answer the questions and be grateful
for the concern? Not to mention that the last thing either of
them needed to hear was someone on the other end of the
line breaking into sobs. Better that Aunt Helen should answer
the phone, or Uncle Jimmy, or Lenore from across the street,
or Tony Vincente.

But Addie took the call from Melanie Sosinski Brown.

The text that reached the older daughter of Anthony Sosinski
while she was on vacation in Maine with her husband was terrifying. Sent by a friend of her father at 9:48 a.m., the message
read only: *Have you heard about your dad and Johnny?* Melanie phoned immediately and got an almost scarier message:

"Somebody" on the *Anna Mary* had gone overboard. The friend did not know who.

Melanie Googled for news. Somewhere on Long Island, she was certain, there was a reporter who could tell her how she could learn firsthand who had gone overboard, when, where, how, and what "gone overboard" meant, but she found no one who could help.

She phoned her younger sister, Emma, in Arizona. She couldn't *not* phone her. As porous as the information was, Emma had to be alerted—even early in the morning, two hours earlier out there.

At the time Emma was waitressing in a bagel café that was in the middle of its morning rush. When the phone first rang, she was busy with a customer and couldn't answer. Three calls later, aware they were from her big sister, Emma decided she had better call back.

The news freaked her out. "We don't know if it's Dad or not," Melanie told her, just that someone had fallen off the boat, and the Coast Guard was surely out there searching. But for Emma, at a distance of two thousand miles, a distance at which even the most trivial event gets magnified, the news was dismaying, especially because this event was in no way trivial. Both women had grown up with an undercurrent of awareness about the dangers of fishing—"You know and you don't want to know," says Melanie. They had heard stories all their lives about the realities of making a living at sea, and they knew that danger was always present. Now it was here, right on top of them.

Emma tried not to panic. Out of some desperate hope she phoned her father, and the call went straight to voicemail.

Her boss told her to go home early. After she got there she kept checking Facebook: she follows so many people from Montauk—it's where she and Melanie grew up, after all—that she thought she would find news there. She didn't.

The sisters' worst fear only had about another hour to run. By around 11:00 a.m. eastern time Melanie decided that the ultimate source for any news must be the Coast Guard, and when she phoned the station in Montauk and established her identity, an officer there confirmed to her that it was Johnny who was missing. Melanie called Emma at once. The relief for both sisters was "overwhelming," in Emma's word, but the disquieting anxiety and the distress weren't entirely relieved. Johnny was like an uncle to both sisters; neither of them could remember a time when Johnny Aldridge and all the Aldridge family were not an integral part of their lives. They thought about Johnny alone and alive—they hoped he was alive—in the ocean, and they thought about what their father was going through aboard the *Anna Mary*.

The Coast Guard officer Melanie had spoken to told her that the Aldridge family had been informed. Melanie tried but failed to find phone numbers for Cathy or Tommy Patterson or for Anthony Aldridge. She wanted a contact in the Aldridge family, a connection to what was happening. But she had long been away from life on Long Island; she had no phone numbers for anyone. She thought it likely that her maternal grandmother in Arizona still had a phone number for the senior Aldridges, and she did. Melanie immediately put in her call to Addie.

They talked for several minutes. Melanie found Addie "obviously distraught" but sweet in the same way Melanie always remembered her to be, the way everybody knew her to be. She was able to tell Melanie that Cathy was on her way to the Montauk Coast Guard station, and she gave her Cathy's number so Melanie had the point of contact she wanted. All Melanie could give her in return was to let Addie know that the Sosinski daughters, from their separate distant locations, were on watch with the Aldridges.

The watch went on. By midday the local television station, *News12 Long Island*, was reporting the bare bones of a story. For Anthony Aldridge, "to hear my brother's name being said on television was an out-of-body experience. All I could think was, 'Oh my God, they didn't ask my permission!'" John Aldridge senior tried not to let the TV reporter's story, boomed out in typical TV reporter fashion, deepen his already profound despair: the television report wasn't telling him anything he didn't already know. But Addie shuddered at hearing the news on television—it somehow made it all the more real.

"Half of Oakdale," Cathy said, had gone to her parents' house, and by now it looked like she had it about right. The senior Aldridges and a number of others were out on the deck at the back of the house, while inside people sat or stood, moving from living room to dining room to kitchen and back again, and still others took over the front steps or huddled on the front lawn. They all knew this comfortable home from front to back—the armchairs that made you want to curl up in them, the family photographs scattered across cheerful pastel walls, the glass cabinet with precious ceramic figurines. Everyone wanted to believe they would be here again as in the past for a cup of coffee at the dining table or a cookout in the backyard or a holiday celebration—and not for the mourning all were trying to keep at bay.

When Helen Battista wandered down to the harbor at about seven that morning shortly after receiving the early-morning text about Load falling off the boat, George Watson was just about the first person she saw. He was on the phone, and he was angry. Someone or other—George forgets who—had flagged down his bicycle minutes before with the news about Johnny's disappearance. Watson was angry because something like that shouldn't happen on a well-run boat like the *Anna Mary*—or on any boat operated by competent commercial fishermen. But even as he swore at whoever he was talking to, he was not particularly worried. "I figured it's okay," Watson says. "Johnny will be fine. I was quite confident they would pick him up"—soon.

That was his early-morning reaction, but as the hours went on, his confidence waned. *Something must have happened*, he thought. *Johnny must've hit his head.* He had complete faith in Aldridge, in his overall abilities and in his skill in handling a boat. That he hadn't been found by midmorning—then by late morning—told Watson that something unknown and untoward was at issue.

George Watson had been running The Dock for forty years that summer of 2013. He had given up a career as one of New York's Bravest—a New York City firefighter—because from his very first visit back when he was a kid, every time he went out to Montauk the one thing he had hated about the place was leaving it. Over the decades he had become as much a part of the Montauk landscape as the Lighthouse on the Point, and if both The Dock and its owner had become must-see tourist attractions, it didn't change the fact that Watson really knows the town, knows its people, knows who the "real Montauk characters" are, even as he has become one of them. He simply cannot imagine living anywhere else in the world, and in his eyes Johnny Aldridge is one of the best things about Montauk—"a stand-up guy everybody loves," says Watson. "He's a fixture out here."

The assumption that underlay his early confidence in Johnny's rescue—the notion that "they would pick him up within an hour or two"—was looking like it was built of wishful thinking. Now some five hours had gone by. It was afternoon. Watson's hopes were in pieces.

George Watson wasn't alone in his growing despair. The Dock, which had opened at noon as usual, was filling up with people for whom hopes of Johnny Aldridge's rescue were sinking into despair. Laurie Zapolski was there for a while, before heading over to Sammys to be with Helen Battista, whose workday would extend until evening. The fishermen who had not been at the harbor in time to go out on search boats were there. Some of the folks who had driven over from Oakdale were there; the Coast Guard Station probably couldn't hold them all. It was an uneasy gathering: the thirty-plus customers George reckoned were there, apart from a few hapless tourists, were friends of Johnny Aldridge. For all of them it was too soon to mourn but too late to tell yourself you were drinking because it was lunchtime, or for the pleasure of it, or because you were thirsty.

The drinkers at The Dock lobbed the same desultory conversation back and forth as did the watchers in the house in Oakdale. After all, what the hell was there to say? The same thing was going on in both landward places: it was not a wake, but it *was* a vigil. And to the people who shared it, it felt like a prayer.

Chapter 12

Cutting Loose

Approximately 11:30 a.m.

I'm holding onto this fixed buoy rope, trying to let my muscles rest after the swim, but it's not all that restful. Every roll of the waves washes over my head, effectively pulling me under. I have to hold my breath and fight swallowing seawater almost as much as if I were swimming. Also, I've become a point of resistance to the waves, so I have to grip the rope pretty hard to hold on. I think the waves may be winning the fight. In any case, I'm getting pounded.

This is not a good spot. It is not a *useful* spot. I thought it would be my salvation. I thought it would give me buoyancy and visibility—let me float and let me get seen. But it's not doing either of those things.

The buoy is too big: I can't get on top of it, and I can't get my arms around it. What I am holding onto is the rope, and the rope attaches through the tapered part of the polyball, which is underwater. So holding onto the rope is not keeping me particularly buoyant—the boots are doing that, and they are doing it better—and I feel like I am holding the string of a balloon. I'm also almost underneath the buoy, so anybody who can see the buoy from the air won't necessarily see me.

The bottom line is that I've killed myself to get here, and I'm not getting what I need from it. But I hold on anyway because at least I am not having to propel myself forward, and I do need to let the muscles in my legs recover, let all my systems get renewed or whatever it is—get the blood flowing to the right places again. I have to reassess, but I have to let some renewal happen first.

And all the time I'm seeing boats go by in the distance, and I hear the helicopter overhead. So I *know* they're looking for me. But it's all happening over there, to the west. The copter is going back and forth, back and forth. He's definitely flying a pattern. What he is *not* doing is flying the pattern over here, where I am. I realize they have concluded that I have been drifting west. They don't know—how could they?—exactly when and where I went overboard, but whatever ideas they've come up with have told them I'm going to be over there, where I quite definitely am not.

I keep holding on.

Then, when I figure I've been here now, holding onto this rope, maybe an hour, hour and a half, I decide that if my blood flow hasn't revived whatever needs reviving by now, hanging on longer is probably not going to make things any better.

So what should I do? Do I stay or go? What's best? My options boil down to these: if I stay, I'm yielding to whatever happens here, where I am far from the search parties and laboring hard to be visible. But if I leave here, I might create another possibility.

Conclusion: I need to be proactive for my own recovery, and I should get the hell out of here. I've got to swim to the next buoy on Pete's line, still farther west.

So think. Assess: What do I have with me for that task? What is my equipment? I have my boots for flotation, my knife, and it is suddenly clear to me that when I leave this spot, I am going to take this buoy with me. This buoy can benefit me, the same as the boots and my knife have benefited me. Anything that can advance my goal I have to keep. I have to keep this buoy because it is a big red ball and more visible than I am in an endless, dark ocean.

But it is a scary thought. I am cutting myself off from the safety—sort of—of a fixed point to head back into an ocean that is always moving, never still, that is churning with energy in the form of waves that batter me and currents that grab and hold me. Cutting myself loose to go back into all that is both scary and exhausting.

Also, figuring out exactly how to *get* the buoy isn't going to be easy. I am still holding onto my boots, one under each arm, tight and close. So it isn't like I have the free use of my arms and hands. A big, red, visible ball the buoy may be, but getting hold of it is going to be tricky.

I am right-handed, so with my right hand, still wearing my sock "mitten," I grab the four- or five-foot rope that tethers the buoy to the main rope anchoring it to the ocean floor.

Now I have to cut that rope, and I need my right hand to do that, so I move the tethering rope to my left hand and use my right to get the knife out of my pocket. I got the boots under my arms; I got the rope in one hand. *Careful,* I tell myself. *I need to be careful.* But I guess I make some sort of awkward move because the boots almost slip out of my grasp. I clutch them tighter, wait for a few seconds to catch my breath, then slide my right hand into my pocket and grip the knife. I am still holding the rope with my left hand, as stretched as I can manage on a swirling, rocking ocean. Now very, very carefully, with the knife in my right hand, I start cutting the tethering rope. I cut as close as I can to the main anchoring rope because I want as much rope as possible to work with, and suddenly, with a jerk, the buoy comes free and pops me up to the surface of the ocean.

What now? I need one arm to hold both boots and the other, my right arm, gloved with my sock, to swim with. There are three-plus feet of buoy rope left, so I put the knife away, clip it securely, then tie the rope around my left wrist with a simple overhand knot; the buoy is now basically locked onto me, tied to my left arm. I start swimming, but I realize very quickly that I cannot swim with the buoy—the ocean swells just won't let me. I also realize that I cannot let the buoy drop behind me when I swim because it will be a drag on my forward notion. What I have to do instead is push the buoy ahead of me. To do that I have to treat it like a balloon. I have to *use* the swells, letting each wave catch the ball and advance it forward. Then I can swim to the ball and push it ahead until the next swell catches it, and then the next and the next.

I know also that I have to plot a trajectory that makes use of the waves in such a way that I can fall onto the next buoy from forward of it. I need to get dragged onto it by the drifting swell. Otherwise, I will shoot past it or behind it or miss it altogether; I won't be able to fight the ocean. I've learned this the hard way, the very hard way, and I'm not going to forget it. What makes the lesson particularly critical is that I don't know what's out there once I pass Pete's buoy. His line of traps is almost like home ground to me, but for all I know, once I'm past his "turf," there may not be any buoys at all. So I can't miss Pete's buoy. It could be my last chance. In other words, this swim matters a whole hell of a lot.

The plan is that I will push the buoy forward the length of the rope tied to my wrist—about three feet—then swim to the buoy. Push it, swim to it. A three-foot goal. And at the top of the water surface, check the direction. I'm figuring one goal a minute.

Time to go.

The plan works pretty much the way I had figured: I am on my side, swimming with my right arm, and a wave comes past my face, grabs the ball tied to my left wrist, and pushes the ball forward. Then I take another sidestroke, and by the time I get to the ball, I'm on the crest of the wave and can catch a visual of my destination. A goal per minute. I go hard for about seven minutes, and then I rest. Ready again, I look up for the buoy, replot my trajectory, then it's head down and swim again.

I have gone maybe an hour and am in the middle of nowhere when I again see the *Anna Mary* up ahead. I am looking at the portside of the boat, and I see Mikey up on the roof staring in my direction through binoculars. I stop, scream, thrust the buoy up in the air, try to splash the water. Why doesn't he see? Why doesn't he notice this totally un-usual buoy, well outside the prescribed area, in a place where no buoy should be? It is irregular, unexpected, not normal—just the sort of thing a searcher should pick up. But it doesn't happen. My boat is right there, not more than four hundred yards away from me, and it steams on by, out of sight.

Stay positive, I remind myself. *Stay positive. They're looking for you. You're not alone if they're looking for you.* I go back to my mission: a goal a minute—push the buoy, swim to the buoy. Three feet forward, every minute.

Minute by minute, this is the longest swim of my life, and a very hard, very painful one. My arms, my legs, every mus-cle is killing me. I feel the fatigue everywhere but especially in my leg muscles—they are locked up in spasms, charley horses. The pain is excruciating, the muscles hardened like rocks. And what can I do about it—stop and stretch? massage the muscles? grab a heating pad? I kick through the charley horses and put the pain aside, just put it aside because *I have to keep swimming*. If whatever leg pain I'm feeling is not kill-ing me, then it just does not fucking matter because I know absolutely that stopping my legs from kicking *will* kill me.

I estimate the swim has taken about two hours when I see the buoy. The northeast trajectory seems just right. I give it everything I've got. Every last bit of strength *now*—reach for the buoy, grab it, hold on. I'm there! I catch my breath while a sense of real accomplishment flows through me. I am fired up. I made it!—and I suddenly think I am Superman. This long, hard, kind of gutsy swim—and I did it.

But with the buoy tied to my wrist, I am still getting pulled under by the waves, and I am tired of it. I want to be on the surface of the water, not fighting its swells and drifts. What if I tie the two buoys together? I slide down the pole of the buoy to the ball, take the rope off my wrist, and knot it to the ball on the new buoy—again with an overhand knot. Then I straddle the rope connecting the two so that I am seated between them.

I am seated and I am not sinking. I am *on* the surface of the ocean, no longer just *at* it, no longer just chinning it and having to fight to keep my head up. For a split second I wonder if I really need the boots now. I think how nice it would be not to have to clutch them every second. But yeah, I need them. They were my indispensable lifeline, and how do I know what's next? Why would I jettison anything until the end, whatever it turns out to be?

I have a better view now. I see the helicopter. I hear boats going up and down. Why aren't they closer? Why don't they come over here and see me?

I feel a small shiver and realize that I am getting a little cold. I'm reminded of why I need the boots. I remember how warm they felt clutched against my chest. The water around me is warm, so I fill the boots with water and hold them close to warm my core. I need to keep my core temperature up, and they act as a kind of wetsuit.

I know that my legs are pretty much spent. The charley horse in both legs was almost unbearable during the swim. I say *almost* because, obviously, I bore it. But it feels like that was the end of my strength, like my legs have no more to give.

I can also feel the skin on my face getting really tight. I know I must be burned all over. This is the first I've thought about sunburn. Not that there was ever anything I could do about it, any more than there is anything I can do about it right now. I want to be seen.

Speaking of seeing, I'm worried also about my eyes. I have glaucoma in my left eye and had surgery maybe a month ago to treat it. Basically the doctor put an implant on the outside of the eye under my eyelid, with a tube that drains the fluid around to the back of the eye in order to decrease the pressure. I have a prescription for drops I'm supposed to be putting in my eye daily; the bottle is somewhere on the *Anna Mary*. I think it is probably safe to say that the salt bath and the sun and everything else I've endured today aren't doing my eyes a lot of good.

The rest of me is okay. Well, it is and it isn't. If I acknowledge my physical deterioration, then I open myself up to the possibility of succumbing to it. That's scary, because if I succumb, then this is the day I die and I have to go all through that mental torture again—all the worry about the lives going on without me in them: my parents' lives, my friends' lives, my nephew Jake's life. The thing is that if I tell myself I am not okay in my body and brain, then dying becomes easy: just sink to the bottom. Staying alive is harder, and I have to believe that I can, that I am okay enough to stay alive. I believe it.

So my assessment right now grades me at unbelievably thirsty and hungry but basically okay. The thirst is pretty intense. I have taken in only seawater and a fair amount of it: as much as I tried not to ingest any, I was up against the constant onslaught of swells and currents that were far more potent than my efforts to keep my head high and dry. There was just no way to avoid ingesting what I've ingested. I think of all the water bottles I've seen floating by when we go out to fish—part of the junk people drop or throw into the ocean. Where is that garbage when I need it? There hasn't been a bit of debris around me since I fell overboard—what? ten hours ago now?

I would kill for a hamburger, of course, but I would also kill—literally, using my knife or my bare hands or my teeth—for any one of these mahi-mahis exploring around me. They light up with many colors, and they are beautiful, and having one to eat would give me protein and moisture, but catching one is out of the question—they are too fast to grab. They're like spectacular lightning strikes of bright color that dart away before I can lift my hand.

Meanwhile Pete Spong is so fastidious about his trawls that he has scraped all the algae off his buoys. They're too clean. There's nothing left on this buoy for me to eat.

I think about swimming home. I do. All day I have thought I would be found and rescued. Now that I'm not fighting anymore, am just hanging on, I have second thoughts. Maybe swimming home is the only way. Can I? I feel that nothing *really* bothers me. I have been in the water for about ten hours, have spent maybe eight hours getting here—why couldn't I swim home in twenty hours?

The answer is in the question: I have been in the water for ten hours already, have expended eight hours' worth of physical energy and who knows how much mental, emotional, psychic energy. The reality is that I cannot swim home in twenty hours. Or ever.

I hold my hand up toward the sun and squint as I count the hand widths between the bottom of the sun and the top of the horizon—a wilderness way to estimate the time until sunset. One, two, three.

If it is going to start getting dark in three hours, I had better not leave this buoy. Floating in the middle of the ocean for a second night would definitely be a bad idea. So okay. Let's just stay here, see what happens.

I'm as visible as I can manage. I am seated between two buoys, and two buoys close together like this constitute a situation that is out of place, unusual, worth taking a look at. I'm still bobbing around like crazy, but I am on the surface of the ocean, not being pulled under. There's nothing to do but think, and my mind turns to all the people I know who have died. Am I going to meet them, or is all of that afterlife stuff just bullshit, as I suspect?

Should I carve or scrape a message in my boots? If I sink and die, the boots will still float and may carry my farewell to my parents. I think what I should say. I would like them to know what happened, but it seems a lot to write. Maybe just say that I tried my best and I love them. I begin scraping at the rubber with my knife, but it doesn't work.

I am going to spend the night here. I see that now. Okay, the thing to do is to set myself up in such a way that I can sleep between the two buoys, and if I fall over, the fall into the water will wake me. The hope is that somebody coming by—some fisherman heading for his traps—will shine a light on this unusual grouping of buoys and will see me. If I am awake, I will say hello, and if I am asleep and drooping, the fisherman will wake me and save me. Except that I know it is possible to become so tired you don't care if you wake up or not, so falling into the water might not be the wake-up call I think it is.

I see the helicopter to the west. Then the fixed-wing jet flies over, relatively close to my position. It is clear he doesn't see me, but it looks like he is flying a pattern. I turn my body the other way on my rope perch, facing him so that I will be looking right at him on his return pass.

He turns, makes the pass. He is coming toward me. He is even closer to me now than before. I am looking right at him, waving. But he doesn't see me this time either.

Chapter 13

Found

2:46 p.m.

The way it works in the MH-60 rescue helicopter is that the SAROPS search pattern from the command center—New Haven, in this case—gets punched into the on-board navigational computer, which then translates the pattern into a flight plan for the guidance system to follow on autopilot. The idea, says Lieutenant Ray Jamros, the pilot of MH-6002, which had launched from Cape Cod air station at 6:30 that morning, is to "minimize the flying work and maximize the searching." Since a little after 7:00 a.m., when the helicopter had arrived at the designated starting point for the first search pattern, four pairs of eyes had been trained on the ocean looking for John Aldridge.

Jamros, copilot Michael Deal, flight mechanic Ethan Hill, and rescue swimmer Bob Hovey had seen a lot of "stuff" in the water that day—turtles, sharks, buoys, all sorts of debris—but nothing resembling a human being, dead or alive. That was the case through four search patterns over a period of more than seven hours in the air. Eight hours is the maximum flight time for the MH-60, so the crew was now at that point when any "landing" would have to be their last. Copilot Deal calculated that the copter was twenty minutes away from "bingo fuel"—military slang for just enough fuel for a safe return to base—and he was on the radio to the New Haven command center asking for a new search pattern.

But the team at New Haven was in a funk. SAROPS had crashed, Rodocker had rebooted and started over, and it would be a couple of hours before the system could come up with a new pattern. That didn't mean that the search stopped—not the Coast Guard's search by boat and plane nor that of the volunteer fleet—but it did mean that a new search pattern incorporating all the latest data was still being processed and was not forthcoming any time soon. Command Duty Officer Mark Averill, conferring with Jonathan Theel just outside the communications suite about plans for extending the search overnight, told Sean Davis to tell the helicopter crew to just "go on home and refuel" and they would start up the search again once SAROPS had a pattern and there was a new crew on a fresh copter. Deal could hear the frustration and weariness in Davis's voice.

"We're approaching fatigue status," Deal argued. "If we go back to base, we're done, but right now we've still got a half hour of fuel, so give us a quick trackline search we can run." He added. "We have absolutely perfect conditions for searching."

It made sense to the Coasties. CDO Averill walked over to the SAROPS monitor, looked over Jason Rodocker's shoulder at the area on the screen where the particles were densest, found the midpoint, noted the latitude and longitude, and in effect drew a straight line with his finger from the helicopter's position east to the boundary of the drift, then four-pointed that line to north and south. The finger drawing produced just what Deal had asked for: a basic trackline search that would take the MH-60 south-southeast through the heart of the search area for ten miles, head it north for ten miles, then veer it north-northwest, boxing off the search and pointing the helicopter toward home on Cape Cod. *There's your pattern*, Averill in effect was saying. *Fly those positions, check the water within that box for thirty minutes, then fly on home.*

"Check the buoys too, if you see any," Averill suggested. "People like to grab onto things if they can." The crew of MH-6002 had been thinking the same thing all day: *Boy, if I were out here, I'd sure look for something to grab onto.*

At 2:46 p.m. they started flying Averill's line, and it was just a few minutes before three when Ray Jamros saw a red ball, saw the pole of the highflyer above it, and saw what looked to him like an arm waving.

"I see him! I got him!" Jamros shouted. "Mark mark mark!"

That was the signal, delivered at two minutes to three on the afternoon of Wednesday, July 24, 2013, for Mike Deal to punch a button annotating the helicopter's current position. He did so as Jamros made a hard, quick turn and came into a hover. First from one hundred feet, then from fifty feet above the surface of the water, the four exhausted, bleary-eyed members of the helicopter crew saw the madly waving, water-pounding, probably screaming-his-lungs-out guy in the water and confirmed that they had found their man. "It was," says Mike Deal, "the greatest feeling in the world." Fatigue fled. The Coast Guard team was energized and in motion.

Within seconds they had run down the rescue checklist. Rescue swimmer Bob Hovey violated regulations and did not take the time to put on the wetsuit he carries in summer. A licensed emergency medical technician, Hovey knew from experience that the relief that can flood an individual who is on the verge of being rescued can lower the person's blood pressure so much he may lose consciousness, and he didn't want to take any more time than absolutely necessary to ready himself. Hovey did switch quickly out of his flight helmet into his swimmer helmet, equipped with mask and snorkel, and he replaced his boots with water shoes over which he fitted his fins.

Hovey also knew that a person in fear of drowning might try to climb onto the rescuer and hold on for dear life, which can endanger both rescuer and the person the rescuer is try-ing to save. So he mentally ticked off the checklist of com-bative swimming skills the Coast Guard had trained him in—ancient martial arts for confronting an enemy in the water so you can both slide out of an unwanted clinch and take control of a person who may be breaking down.

Helmeted, finned, but still in his flight suit, Hovey was ready, just waiting now for the helicopter to get into the right position.

Chapter 14

"It's Over"

2:58 p.m.

The jet that passed me by is long gone. I am back to staring at a faraway helicopter that is looking for me the same way the song says a lot of us look for love—in all the wrong places. The minutes are ticking by, and the day is growing older. Ten minutes pass. Twenty. Thirty minutes. Forty minutes. I'm thinking how I will rope myself to the highflyer in some way so that, if the worst should happen, there will be a body my family can bury. I don't want to just sink to the bottom and never be found.

I am feeling cold now, and I am a little afraid I may fall asleep. *Take a nap and die*, I think. So I try hard to stay awake.

I hear again the big thundering sound of the helicopter, and it seems not so far away anymore. It seems to be coming toward me. Actually it *is* coming toward me. It is coming right down the barrel at me. I throw one boot in the air and start smacking the water with my hands and with the boot. I am splashing, I am waving like crazy, and I am screaming my lungs out. Stupidly. Because who can hear anything in this noise?

Now the helicopter is hovering above me. It is stopped above me. I can read USCG on the bottom of it, and I see a guy peering out the open door on the side of the cabin. They see me!

It's over. I'm going to be saved. It's really over now. I take a deep breath—such a deep breath.

The helicopter moves off because the rotor wash is so violent it could plow me under. It hovers even lower, and just as I turn my back, I see the guy harnessed onto the cable and coming down out of the door. I wait for him. He taps me on the shoulder. "Sir," he says, loud and clear, "I am a Coast Guard rescue swimmer, can you turn around for me?" I do as he asks. I'm looking at him, and I know I have my life back.

I think he asks me if I'm okay, if I'm injured, if I can let go of my boots so they don't turn into dangerous projectiles.

"Am I okay?" I shout. "Hell, I've got two more days left in me."

But I really don't, and when the guy tells me, "Sir, we're in control now. Don't worry. We'll take care of everything," every muscle in my body just unclutches, just eases and lets go. The relief feels like a warm, golden liquid running through every vein and capillary in my whole body, from my brain to my core to my toes and into every fingertip. I'm just limp, only vaguely aware that my boots are floating away.

The swimmer grips me in a body tow around the neck, and I remember the boots.

"My boots!" I say to him. "They saved my life. Can we get them?"

He hesitates maybe a second. "Sure," and he swims me over, grabs the boots, and hands them to me, then swims me over to the extraction point.

Now the guy is raising his arm, palm inward, signaling to the guy I can see hanging out the side of the helicopter, and the basket is being lowered over the side. "Sir," my rescuer says to me—never in my life have I been addressed so formally so many times—"we are going to hoist you into the helicopter, and I want to warn you there will be extreme rotor wash that will feel like BBs fired at your face, so turn away from it." He pauses. "Very important also: keep your arms and legs inside the basket, and when it starts swinging, just relax. The flight mechanic up there will deal with it."

The basket lands right next to me on the water surface. I'm thinking: *Not only is the Coast Guard saving me, but they're doing it with pinpoint accuracy.*

The swimmer rolls me into the basket. "Keep your hands inside no matter how much the basket swings, and just hold on," he says, and then I am being reeled up. I am blown away because I have been saved, but even so, when I get up above two stories high, swinging in midair in that basket, I have to close my eyes. I don't ride roller-coasters either.

The next thing I know, the flight mechanic is hauling the basket into the cabin, then is rolling me out of the basket onto my knees. I manage to sit, and the flight mechanic sends the hook back down. I tell the copilot, "Please, you've got to call my boat." He hands me a headset. I hear him telling the command center to try to raise Anthony. "*Anna Mary, Anna Mary*, come in. This is the Coast Guard."

"Coast Guard, this is *Anna Mary*." It is Anthony's voice. Unmistakable.

"*Anna Mary*, we have John Aldridge. He is alive and well."

"You got him? You got him? He's alive?"

I can hear the elation and the relief in Anthony. I can even hear the rolling shouts and cheers from captains he is connected to down the line. I have only a headset, so I can't reply, nor do I have the strength or the will for such a conversation just yet. But it doesn't matter at all right now.

From the cockpit the copilot tosses me a bottle of water. "You have got some will to live," he says to me, but I can't get the water down my throat. My whole mouth feels completely swollen. I seem to be able to talk, however. "I got too many people who love me to die," I tell the copilot.

Then the swimmer is back up in the cabin, and we are heading off. I feel great, am totally fired up. I must appear to be completely out of control to these guys, who don't seem to be able to believe they're talking to me. They are all my rescuers, and I get their names—Ray and Mike, pilot and copilot working the controls in the cockpit, and back in the cabin with me, blond, bespectacled Ethan, the flight mechanic, and dark-haired Bob, the swimmer who came and got me. "Sorry we can't get you to Montauk," Hovey says to me. "We have to take you to Cape Cod."

I am dehydrated and very cold, and I can feel my swollen, salt-encrusted, burned-to-a-crisp face beaming from ear to ear. "I don't give a shit where you take me," I tell them, and the guys laugh. Cape Cod, Cape Hatteras, Cape of Good Hope— any cape or no cape for all I care. I can't believe what a class act these Coast Guard guys are: they send boats and planes and whatever to pull me out of the water, and then they apologize for not taking me to my front door. I'm alive, I'm saved, I'm going home, I have my whole life back, and I am wild with excitement. Psyched! Psyched to be alive, psyched to be in this helicopter. I'm looking out the window, and I'm answering the questions the guys are asking. The adrenaline is racing through me, but this is a whole other kind of adrenaline—not the kind from twelve hours ago, when I was sure I was going to die and the adrenaline rush was from terror, my heart beating out of my chest in such a scary way. This adrenaline is a rush of euphoria. It is intense, and it is not subsiding. I feel so good.

The guys are asking me questions about what happened and what it was like to be in the water. "Were you really there for twelve hours?" one of them asks. "Yeah, but you know, it wasn't so bad," I hear myself say.

"Do my parents know I fell overboard?" I ask, and when they nod yes, I joke with them, "Fuck!" I say. "My mother is going to kill me!" But what I'm thinking is that anger is not at all what she has been going through. I don't really want to think about what she and my father have been going through.

"Can I get a selfie?" Hovey asks, bringing my mind back to where I am. I shiver. As sunburned as I am, I feel cold. Somebody wraps me in a blanket, and the copilot, Mike Deal, takes a photo of me. I'm just a guy everybody is hanging out with, and neither they nor I can believe it.

We're coming into the Coast Guard air station at Cape Cod, and I see an ambulance on the tarmac. There are maybe a dozen Coasties standing in a formation, and there is another stack of people over on the left. This is my first inkling that my disappearance has had a wider impact than on just me and Anthony.

I put my boots on so I don't have to carry them when we land, but the truth is, I cannot walk. The skin on the inside of my thighs is rubbed raw from sitting on the rope, and my leg muscles, understandably, are on strike. The crew that saved me grabs me under the arms and walks me to the ambulance. Cameras click, lights flicker, and then I am on my back in the ambulance, where they tell me that my core temperature is 94—no wonder I'm cold.

I am wheeled into the hospital entrance, into an area that is like the triage room, and the place is chaos. I suppose it's because it is high summer on Cape Cod, and people are probably doing all sorts of stupid things that land them in the hospital—not unlike me. Everybody is on a cell phone, and I ask a total stranger if I can borrow his—I need to call my mother.

Like everybody else, I really don't know anybody's phone number anymore—except my mother's. To make a call, I mostly just push a button next to a name. I also know that neither of my parents ever answers the phone if they don't recognize the number of the person calling. My mother won't recognize this number, but I figure I'll take a chance.

She answers. "Hello?"

"Ma! Did you miss me?" She bursts into tears. "Ma," I say, "you didn't think you'd get rid of me so easily, did you?"

"How are you?" my mother asks me.

"I'm fine, totally fine."

"Are you all right? How are you?" I can tell that my mother is only half listening to the words. All she can hear is my voice, that I'm alive. That's okay. I get that. That I'm really alive is all she needs to know.

"Ma, I'm really fine. Really. You know, the boots saved my life."

"That's good. It's so good to hear your voice. How are you? Are you sure you're okay?" She is mouthing these words. She doesn't care. She just wants to hear me.

"I'm sure. Really."

I give back the phone because I am suddenly being wheeled into a room where the medics go to work on me. Tests, more tests, IVs pumping warm fluids into me. My sunburn equates to a second-degree burn, they tell me. My retinas are burned, and I have rope burns and a rash under my arms—probably from clutching the rubber boots. The ice cube they give me because I am so thirsty burns my tongue and the roof of my mouth painfully. Another hour and a half passes before I can swallow.

The hospital is so crowded that they wheel me out of the room—which I guess they need for somebody really sick—into a hallway near the nurses' station. I lie there with my IVs, waiting for my hydration levels to get right. Nobody comes near me. Nobody rinses me off or changes my clothes or anything. I finally flag down somebody heading for the nurses' station to complain about the rope burns. "Can you find me a salve or something?" I beg. A nurse comes at last with a cooling cream.

This also seems to remind the staff to move me again. "We've got a room for you," the orderly or whatever says, as he pushes me into what looks like a storage closet with a lot of crutches hanging from the walls. At least it's quiet.

Then I get a visit from the hospital press liaison. There's a reporter here from *Newsday*, the Long Island newspaper— would I talk to her? Sure. Happy to. She comes upstairs into my little storage closet, and I tell her my story.

Chapter 15

Saved

3:05 p.m.

"They got him!"

Sean Davis blurted out the news being blurted out to him from the MH-60 helicopter, and the watchstanders in the New Haven command center, to a man, stood, cheered, and high-fived one another.

"Let's confirm that," said CDO Mark Averill, although he too was smiling. No way Averill was going to report to his boss, Jonathan Theel, until he was sure Aldridge was alive, well, and in Coast Guard hands. Nor, he knew, would Theel report to the Aldridge family unless he had absolute certainty that the report was true.

But Davis's shout over the radio was also heard in the glass-walled communications suite in the Coast Guard station in

Montauk, where Jason Walter, the officer in charge of the station, now back from patrol in the small response boat and trying to juggle the demands of the numerous constituencies on site at the station, also wanted the facts confirmed. For one thing, Walter knew from experience that there can actually be many a slip between spotting a person in the water and getting that person safe and sound into a helicopter and en route to a medical facility. He was aware of stories about individuals who were found alive, then died in the basket or in the helicopter because the stress to their bodies had simply been too great.

Compounding this hesitation was the fact that some twenty family members and friends of John Aldridge and Anthony Sosinski were on the porch—tense, stressed, grieving. Reporters from various news outlets were starting to call the station, asking for "status updates." And local law enforcement officials continued to look over the Coasties' shoulders, ready to "assist" and/or take over the operation at a moment's notice. The bottom line was that Jason Walter was not going to make a move until he heard something more definite than "Sounds like a helicopter got him!"

He called the New Haven command center.

By this time Averill had confirmed to Theel and to Commander Heather Morrison, the officer in charge of Sector Long Island Sound, that Aldridge was indeed alive and well, cold but responsive, elated to have been saved, and on his way to air station Cape Cod for transfer to the hospital. Theel asked Averill again whether Mark was sure about the news, and he admits that Averill's assurances gave him goosebumps and sent him pretty much running into the command center to join the cheering.

He then got on the phone to Montauk Station and instructed Jason Walter to bring the family inside the building
and to put the phone on speaker. Walter told himself that if
it was going to be on speaker, it had to be good news, but of
course, he couldn't be sure. He headed out to the porch, approached Cathy, and asked if she and the other family members would please come into his office—Commander Theel
from the command center in New Haven needed to speak
with them.

That's when Cathy got scared. She called for Tommy, who
was down at the station dock. He came running up the lawn
to the porch where she could grab onto him if she needed to.
The four of them—Cathy, Tommy, Jillian, and Teresa walked
inside. Cathy remembers a long walk down a long hallway into
Walter's private office, not unlike the storied long walk of the
condemned waiting to hear their fate. They stood in a circle
around the desk and waited while Walter clicked the phone
onto the speaker setting. You could have heard a pin drop in
that room as they listened to Jonathan Theel, with military
formality, introduce himself. Cathy thought at first that she
was hearing a rote recitation: name, rank, and serial number
kind of thing—like something out of a manual of operations.
Then Theel said, "We have located John Aldridge"—he rattled
off the coordinates of where—"and he is alive and well." Cathy
almost didn't hear what came after that, which was Theel saying that Johnny was on his way to Cape Cod for medical treatment—it hadn't been possible to fly him back to Montauk.

Cathy, Tommy, Jillian, Teresa all did what people do when
they are joyful: they yelled and wept and hugged one another, relief serving as simultaneously a balm and a trigger to

excitement. The Coasties joined in the elation; it was a good day all around for Station Montauk. Earlier in that afternoon, when she realized that no one had eaten a thing all day, Cathy had dispatched Tommy's partner, Rob Howard, for pizza. The food arrived in the middle of the party and was shared between Coasties and civilians.

Theel had requested that Cathy wait five minutes before phoning her parents or informing anyone else. It was a duty he felt the Coast Guard owed John and Addie Aldridge, especially as he had been the one to bring them the awful news that morning. Cathy acceded to the request.

But Theel's call came maybe a beat too late. At the Oakdale house Uncle Jimmy got a text from a fellow law enforcement retiree who had heard the news over the network of signals that connects all former cops. Theel's call confirmed for John and Addie and the vigil keepers in Oakdale what Uncle Jimmy's shout had presaged: their boy was alive and well.

Cathy waited the five minutes she had promised, then sent a broadcast text to the ninety or so people she had been hearing from all morning. At The Dock, at Sammys, around the harbor, all across the East End, at a vacation spot in Maine, and in a young woman's home in Arizona, cheers erupted as the message was received.

Cathy, Tommy, Jillian, and Teresa headed for Johnny's apartment in Montauk. There they retrieved clean clothes for him and drank cold beer from his fridge. Then they set off for Cape Cod.

After the ambulance took John Aldridge away, the air crew of helicopter MH-6002 waited for the fixed-wing aircraft to return to base, then all of them debriefed together. They also connected with the SAR team at the New Haven command center. The discussion was about how things could have gone better: in the military services, they always need to figure out how things could have gone better. The discussion went on for a while—there was a lot to say.

But the businesslike briefing, the ticking-off of points on an agenda, was not enough to dim the emotions stirred in the MH-6002 crew, the four guys who had found and extricated Aldridge with such smoothly efficient professionalism. For Ethan Hill the experience of having found Johnny alive and well was "a jolt of energy," and talking with him even briefly—notoriously difficult in the very noisy cabin of the helicopter—was "awesome." To copilot Mike Deal, shaking Aldridge's hand was "one of the proudest moments I've had in the US Coast Guard." It's safe to say that Jamros and Hovey felt the same.

Most of the crew members who had participated in the rescue in one way or another got home in time to see the full story reported on the nightly news and to consider the effort they had made and the impact it had had on a human life. The next morning each of them was back on duty.

John Sosinski got off the bus from the Senior Center at around three that afternoon, same as every Monday through Friday during those months when he and Anthony are in Montauk. Once back in the house, he looked forward, as is his habit, to the four o'clock news on television that would fill him in on the day's events. But before the news got started, his granddaughter Emma called him. She filled him in on the one event of that day that came so close to John Sosinski's life. "Daddy's okay," she assured him. "Johnny is alive, and Daddy is on the *Anna Mary*, and he's fine."

The call was another smart move on Emma's part. The first image on the four o'clock news that day was of Johnny Aldridge being hoisted into the helicopter. Had he not received the call from Emma, John Sosinski's first thought would have been: *What happened to my son and where's the boat?*

His son was on the boat, and he was bringing it home.

Mike Skarimbas was still on his mission of searching when the call came over the VHF that Johnny had been found. "I bawled," Skarimbas says simply. Earlier Skarimbas had been concerned when the Coast Guard instructed the volunteer fleet to turn east, questioning the decision in his mind while carrying it out anyway. *Nothing here goes east*, he thought to himself. But even learning that Johnny had been found west of where he had been instructed to go, he couldn't have cared less. He did not care where, how, or by whom the rescue had come about. His best friend was safe, and Mike Skarimbas bawled.

"Because it's not supposed to work that way," says Skarimbas. "It always, *always* works the other way. This was a total anomaly. A total anomaly." He pauses. "It was the worst day of my life, and it became the best day of my life."

Close to ten o'clock that night the *Anna Mary* and the vessels of the volunteer fishing fleet pulled back into Montauk harbor. That was maybe a good thing for Anthony—the delay gave him time to "come down" from the emotional peak he had been climbing since six in the morning when Mike woke him and told him Johnny was gone. His physiology had gone haywire—first with chills, then with sweating that poured off his body, then with the taste of acid in his mouth all day long. He had pushed all the emotion down somewhere—maybe that was why the sweat came out of his feet—to do what he had to do during the search. At the time Johnny was found he was steaming east to the other side of the volunteer fleet, calculating that if Johnny had been drifting for somewhere between eight and ten hours at a half a knot per hour, that is where he might be. His mind was on the conditions and on making use of the hours of daylight still left for finding his partner.

Learning that the Coast Guard had him was as much a jolt to the system as learning he was lost—just much, much better. He was, he said, "over the top."

He likens the physical effect to the sensation he once felt when he was vacationing out West and took a helicopter ride through the Grand Canyon. "The lift-off, following the first little lift-up, is a shock to the system," he says, "a physical sensation to the body. I can't explain it, but this was similar. It was a lift-off I felt in my body."

A crowd of some forty or more people awaited Anthony and Mike Migliaccio and the rest of the volunteer fleet at the town dock that night, Nancy Atlas among them. The waiting crowd formed a rope line for the returning captains and crews to walk through to applause and hugs. The loudest applause and the tightest hugs were for Anthony. Atlas remembers one big, burly guy crying, grabbing Anthony in a hug, telling the crowd how well Anthony had coordinated the volunteer fleet and how important that work was. The Coast Guard agreed. Jason Walter would state officially that "the fishing crews allowed us to search a much greater area," thereby contributing significantly to the eventual rescue.

Anthony and Mike, once Johnny's rescue had been confirmed and they were heading for home, had put out their lines and caught two tuna, which Anthony filleted neatly as the *Anna Mary* steamed toward the harbor. Now, on the town dock in Montauk, Anthony gave away chunks of very fresh Atlantic tuna to the folks greeting him.

There was a moon that night too—"magnificent," says Atlas, "almost reddish, very still, beautiful." She took a good, slow look at the moon, then joined everybody heading into The Dock to celebrate.

Chapter 16

The Good Daughter

July 25, 2013

My sister arrived at the hospital late last night—close to midnight, in fact—along with Tommy and Jillian and Teresa. They had driven up from Montauk, where they had been at the Coast Guard station since early morning. They started up here at about 4:00 or 4:30 yesterday afternoon, with basically just the clothes they were wearing. No cash, no gas in the car, not even a toothbrush. The trek from Montauk was quite a trip: they had to take three ferries, and when they finally arrived, they weren't even sure which hospital to go to. Cathy's first time on Cape Cod ever—not exactly a luxury vacation trip. Cathy didn't care. She seemed almost lightheaded, freed from the weight of worry I knew she had been carrying. They all seemed incredibly happy and free. I was so glad to see them.

They headed off for their motel, and I tried to sleep. I already knew from a couple of other experiences that hospitals are not a great place for that. There's so much going on all the time, plus the lights in the hall, nurses coming in to check my IVs, noise. I think I got almost no sleep. Then this morning the doctors come in and tell me I'm fine; I can leave. To prove it, they wheel me out of my storage closet into the waiting area at the hospital door. Thank God Cathy has left me her cell phone. I punch in Tommy's number and tell them to come and get me as soon as possible. Cathy and all of them had just sat down to have breakfast at some diner and are blown away by the news. *Eat fast*, I beg: the waiting area is even more chaotic than when I arrived last night, partly because the PR people are now fielding all sorts of questions about me.

They must have wolfed down their food, because pretty soon they all walk in the hospital door, and we are ready to go. I sort of automatically get in the front seat of the car, next to Tommy who is driving. It's the roomiest seat, yes, but with my burned skin and scraped groin and aching muscles, I figure it's the best spot for me. But it means the three women share the backseat, which is probably not all that comfortable, and it also means, obviously, that I have my back to them—to the woman I've been in a relationship with, to my sister-in-law who has been unbelievably supportive, and to my sister to whom I owe so much, although I still haven't learned the full extent of her strength in all this.

So this is how I ride home after very nearly drowning in the ocean: sort of distancing myself from two key members of my family as well as from a relationship that both of us in it pretty much know is not working. In a way it's kind of the perfect return to "normalcy." What could be more normal than putting up with discomfort—physical on the part of the three women, of whom I am very fond, in the backseat, emotional discomfort in my case—throughout a trip lasting five hours? That's five hours if there's no traffic—and in the summer on the Massachusetts and Connecticut coasts, not to mention across Long Island, what are the chances of that?

Still, I find myself staring out the window at the scenery passing by with something like the awe I felt looking out of the helicopter yesterday. I'm still trying to absorb being alive and being "back." I don't talk much, I guess.

The traffic isn't too bad—even on a Thursday most people are heading *to* the Cape while we are getting the hell away from it. We get to New London in a couple of hours. From here we'll take the ferry across Long Island Sound to Orient Point on the North Fork of the island, then head west and south for Oakdale. At the ferry station I run into the *Newsday* reporter who interviewed me last night, Nicole Fuller. She is also heading home.

New London is the departure point for lots of different ferries—to Block Island, to Fishers Island, to Martha's Vineyard. But the ferry to Orient Point leaves every half hour, so we don't have long to wait. On board, we all head straight for the bar, although all I can drink is water, which I am grateful to be able to swallow. People are looking at me like they recognize me. It is a very odd sensation.

The ferry takes about an hour and a half, and when we arrive there's a news crew on the dock. I find out also that the news people have been onto the family—my father has been quoted on CBS and in *Newsday*. I have talked to him by phone as well. I think he is doing okay, but I really want to see everyone in person. That's how I'll know they're doing okay.

Back in the car, we're less than an hour away from him and my mother and whoever else is at the house. I'm really ready to get there. I want to see my parents, or rather, I want them to see me—to give them the absolute assurance that I am alive and well and in the house I grew up in. We get to the top of the street and look down it, and there must be fifteen, maybe twenty news vans pulled up in front of my parents' house. Microphones, wires, satellite dishes—the scene looks like something out of a sci-fi movie.

Cameras whir and reporters shout as the car pulls into our driveway. I am halfway out of the car when my nephew Jake just leaps into my arms, and some kind of an interrupted yelp comes out of his mouth. "Jakie, boy," I'm saying. "Jakie boy." I can see my parents coming toward me, and a second later my father has his arms around me in a tight grip. "It wasn't real till now," he says. My mother is hugging Cathy, who is saying something to her, and now my mother has come over to hold me. Then it's my brother, Anthony. He is my baby brother, but he is bigger than I am, and I think his grip is tighter than my father's was—now we're holding one another up. No words. Words aren't needed. Just gripping and breaths held and you know the phrase "tears of joy"? Here they were.

The cameras are still whirring, and the reporters are all still there. I pick up Jake and hold him in my arms while I tell the assembled reporters this, that, whatever—I'm glad to be home, it feels good, the boots saved me, are we done here? The boots, true, but also, as I've already told my sister, it was thinking about not seeing Jake grow up that really kept me going.

I go into the house. There are so many people there, and more are on the way.

More news people are on the way too. After a while I go outside again and answer some more questions from this new batch. Actually the questions are the same as those asked by the old batch, and my answers are pretty much the same too. I begin to wonder how many times they can keep asking and I can keep answering the same words. Boots. Coast Guard. Family. It's what everyone wants to hear: not wanting to let my family down is what kept me alive. Already a narrative has been set up and locked in.

Back in the house a party has erupted—and it's a good one. I'm a little overwhelmed to realize how many people have been affected by the idea of me dying. I know it's a cliché, but I can't help feeling that you just don't realize how much you're loved until you go through something like this. Also, I think that coming so close to losing everything maybe lets me understand loss a little better. I look at my parents, and I find myself measuring the size of what they feared they were losing. I know I can't quite compute it, but having been through what I've been through lets me come close. I'm feeling over-joyed but also unsettled.

These are not the most party-like thoughts. Also, I don't think I slept at all last night, and I know I didn't sleep the night before. It's Thursday night, and I've basically been awake since Tuesday morning. I'm probably exhausted. I am also feeling a bit crowded by all the attention, which is kind of the last thing I need right now. So I signal my sister Cathy that I need to get out of here, and we take off for her place. She keeps a bedroom for me there, and on this occasion there are also flowers, balloons, and champagne on the porch.

We both figure it is okay that we left the party. After all, Cathy had dutifully done what our mother asked of her: she brought me home.

Chapter 17

Postscripts and Parties

Summer's End, 2013

That night, lying in bed in his sister's house but still not sleeping, Johnny heard a knock on the door. It was Anthony. Johnny shot out of bed and the two men hugged. "You okay?" Anthony asked. "I'm okay," Johnny said. The exchange was typically perfunctory, but equally typically, both men knew what they meant.

Anthony scrutinized his partner. He really did look okay. Granted, his face was burned and his nose was peeling. But he was there, alive.

"How are your eyes?" Anthony asked.

"Okay." Then Johnny added, "I'm tired."

"Yeah, you would have to be," Anthony said. The man's body was on day four of no substantive sleep. He had to be totally exhausted, and he was still in shock from just being alive.

Anthony, by contrast, was intensely awake and could barely contain his joy. In Cathy Patterson's house that night, he felt, in his words, that he was "looking at a dead man." Throughout the prior day he had sensed in his gut that he would never see Johnny again. All day he kept hearing in his head the final scream of Joe Hodnik, the young fisherman whose drowning had spurred the creation of the Lost At Sea Memorial on Montauk Point. Even as he worked the VHF and checked coordinates and handed out assignments to the volunteer fleet, Anthony kept seeing in memory that empty black water where Hodnik and Ed Sabo had gone down so many years before. Chubby Gray wasn't far from his thoughts either—the young man from Maine whose boat was the twin of the *Anna Mary* and who had been lost at sea just seven months before. Anthony had known both these men when they were young and vital, and their terrifying loss hovered above his heart all day, fueling the near certainty, reinforced by everything he knew about the ocean and all his experience of life, that Johnny was gone. To now be in the same room with the living Johnny Aldridge was a relief so deep that he felt his heart singing.

He did not stay long. "Get some sleep," he told Johnny.

The next day, Friday, Johnny Aldridge went out to lunch at McGovern's Bar & Grill, an Oakdale institution, to eat the hamburger he had fantasized about when he was in the water, clinging to a buoy for dear life.

By prearrangement his sister Cathy texted the location of the lunch to Laurie Zapolski, who showed up to announce to Johnny, "I need a hug."

She got it.

The impromptu gathering at the home of the senior Aldridges the night of Johnny's return had not entertained a big enough crowd nor, in the eyes of many, had it been a sufficiently substantive celebration of what had occurred. There was still a lot of steam left in the kettle.

The valve was opened first with an Oakdale party on Saturday night, July 27, 2013. This party was by and for the community—the friends, neighbors, and family members Johnny had grown up with. The location was two barges tied together on the Connetquot River—enough room for the partygoers, the "supplies," and the band. Said band, well known along the south shore and around the East End, was the Bedrockers, and it's probably safe to say that lead singer Laurie Zapolski and guitarist Anthony Vincente performed like never before, that they sang and played their hearts out. Just about the whole town was there—one or two may have been sick in bed—and just about everyone in attendance wore a T-shirt with the legend "Load Lives" on the back. Drinks flowed, barbecue sizzled, and the band played song after song. There was something very real to be very happy about, and just in case anyone needed a reminder, about an hour into the party a plane flew overhead trailing a huge sign that read "Welcome Home Johnny Load. Rock, Lobster." The sign was courtesy of

Vinny Passavia, an old family friend who had hired the plane. The party went on into the wee hours.

So did the beach party in Montauk two days later, on Monday, July 29. This one was on the bay side of Montauk, on the Navy Road beach, and it pretty much belonged to the Montauk fishing fraternity. There must have been two hundred people there that day—hosted by Anthony and Mike Migliaccio. Lots of veterans of the volunteer fleet were there, folks who had gone out looking for Johnny just a few days before. The music was by local musicians like Joe Delia and Thomas Muse, with Muse's wife, Nancy Atlas herself, performing on the deck of the *Anna Mary*, which was backed up to the beach. The beach itself was packed with stoves and hibachis cooking up a storm and with coolers filled to the brim with drinks, all of it being consumed at all times. There was even an ice luge—a huge block of ice down which liquor could be poured into the waiting mouth of whoever was thirsty at that moment.

There wasn't even a puff of steam still to be let out after this party. For Montauk, that is saying something . . .

Afterward Johnny and Anthony went back to work.

By October the relationship with Teresa was over. Johnny and Laurie reconnected, and she gave him an ultimatum: this time we either have to be all-in-and-forever, or forget it.

They took the all-in-and-forever option.

In December of that momentous year, on the supposedly unlucky Friday the Thirteenth, a contrarily auspicious event took place at the Montauk Fire Department. There the commander of the US Coast Guard's Sector Long Island Sound, Captain Edward J. Cubanski, presented to the members of Coast Guard Station Montauk the service's Meritorious Team Commendation for the station's part in the rescue of John Aldridge. On hand for the ceremony were the members of the Coast Guard who had been present on July 24 and involved, one way or another, in the rescue effort; Aldridge himself; Anthony Sosinski; and all those captains and crew members of the volunteer fleet who could make it that evening. The award citation spoke of the Coasties' "devotion to duty" and "outstanding performance," and all present were aware that the same words applied to the fishermen who went out looking for their man, to Sosinski, and to the man himself.

Epilogue

Three years after he spent six hours of one day fearing his son had drowned, John Aldridge senior told an interviewer he hadn't had a full night's sleep since that day. Every night when he closes his eyes he expects he will wake up at some point in the night to the same old nightmare—the one he lived through on July 24, 2013.

His wife says she no longer relives the experience every day, as she did for a long time after the event, but when something triggers the memory, she has to remind herself that her son Johnny is alive and well and living his life.

Both of them worry more than they used to about his fishing trips. John senior confesses that he will phone his son the day after a trip, and if it rings once, he will hang up, with the ring itself serving as evidence that the phone is okay and therefore so is Johnny.

For the first week after she brought her brother home Cathy Patterson had stomach pains; it took days before the stress wore off. She also called her brother at least once a day for three weeks until a friend told her she was driving him crazy. Today she says she doesn't worry about her brother when he's out at sea, but the emotional scar she wears is very raw. The mention of the day he fell overboard is enough to start her tears flowing. A glimpse of the Coast Guard station's porch on a visit to Montauk will do the same.

For youngest sibling Anthony, the trauma simply never goes away. "There is not one day of my life that I don't think about what happened back then," he says. "I think about it all the time." Anthony is the baby of the family, the kid brother. Anybody who has ever looked up to an older sibling will understand what he is saying. It's not that he worries about Johnny—although he knows the danger of being on the water, he is confident in his brother's proven ability to survive. But every day he relives what he calls "the worst day of my life" and the startling moment when he "could actually feel what it was like that Johnny had died." Johnny himself tells Anthony to "get a grip," but he can't. This isn't a memory Anthony can put aside. "It's branded in my mind," he says, burned indelibly into his brain.

Laurie Zapolski, now Johnny's life partner for real, says the memory of the day Johnny went overboard arrives unexpectedly and for no reason she can discern, that it runs like a movie in her head, and that it stops her cold.

Talk to Johnny's friends—from kindly Helen Battista to crusty cynic George Watson to devoted Mike Skarimbas, from Oakdale pal Pat Quinn now three thousand miles away in Oregon to Tony Vincente still right there in Oakdale, all those friends who've seen life from all sides by now—and mention the day Johnny went missing, then watch for the tears to start. You won't wait long.

The experience never fully leaves any of them.

That is natural. Entirely recognizable. The psychic manifestation of posttraumatic stress disorder—PTSD—is a phenomenon everyone has heard about.

Statistically, of course, the chances of another fishing or boating mishap ever again happening to Johnny Aldridge are virtually nil. Moreover, Johnny Aldridge is fine. He is alive and well and back where he wants to be and doing the work he loves. But statistics and logic do not matter in this case. Flashbacks—the sudden remembering that retriggers the nightmare—are a cardinal sign of PTSD, a classic indication that the individual is reliving the event and the distress it produced.

Unexpected, unforeseen, unrealistic—in every way imaginable Johnny Aldridge's falling overboard was all of those things. This is a man who takes no chances with the unexpected, who consistently makes preparations against the unforeseen, who has little or no patience with unreality. Meticulous in his commitment to all the details of his work, Johnny Aldridge is known as a guy who follows the checklist. You can set your watch by it.

Then he goes and yanks at a plastic handle that instantly comes apart, and the universe that you suspected was held together by toothpicks anyway is utterly shattered. It is shattered because you knew, everybody knew, above all *he* knew that this was a possibility. He knew that the handle was loose, and when the guy who never lets a detail get past him lets this detail get past him, the world that was once safe and predictable for all of us gets thrown totally out of whack. That is the nightmare that comes back to haunt people who suffer from the flashbacks again and again: it's the nightmare in which you say to yourself, *You mean the ground I am standing on could give way at any second?*

Occurrences of these nightmares and flashbacks may persist for some time—months, years, decades. They can fade eventually, although for some people they may stick around forever. Trauma accumulates, and who knows what underlying layers of trauma in any one individual's brain Johnny's incident may be piling onto. Or, in the case of parents and siblings, it may be that six hours of visualizing life without Johnny was just too viscerally disastrous. For those folks, a "cure" may take some time.

The two protagonists in the story who are suffering no flashbacks, no nightmares, no real evidence of posttraumatic stress at all are Anthony Sosinski and Johnny Aldridge himself. Anthony says it is simply not in his nature to be hung up on what is past and can no longer be changed. He has always been a man who sees the glass as half full and is glad of what his life is rather than pondering or worrying over what might have been. He has seen his share of loss and casualty. He has, as he says, pulled enough bodies out of the water and suffered the loss of enough friends to supply anxiety for a lifetime.

This is not to suggest, however, that Anthony has forgotten that day or the loss that for so many hours seemed so very real. He never forgets it, and the memory never fails to hurt. Years after the fact, just reading an industry report that

unwitnessed, man-overboard fatalities "are especially preva-
lent in the northeastern lobster fishery" can make his whole
body shudder all over again.*

The upshot, however, is that Anthony feels lucky—to be
alive, to be the father of healthy children whose achievements
have surpassed all his wildest expectations; to have a house,
to be able to take care of his father, to be a partner in the
Anna Mary, and to go fishing for a living. He is not a man to
dwell on what almost happened on July 24, 2013. His concern
is the here and now.

As for Johnny Aldridge, maybe one reason he escapes the
nightmares and flashbacks is that he's the guy that lived the
experience and therefore worked through it—beginning,
middle, end—in real time. It is memory for him, not a bad
dream. Perhaps for that same reason the boots that saved his
life are still in his closet—and always will be.

He remembers telling the Coasties in the helicopter that
the twelve hours in the water "wasn't so bad." It was a dumb
thing to say, yet he can see that same idea on some people's
faces when they look at him. He knows they're thinking:
*Twelve hours in the ocean on a calm day? How tough could
it have been*? He wants to say to them: *You try swallowing
ocean water for twelve hours, then come back and tell me how
you like it.* He remembers the battle waged in his brain for
twelve hours between giving in and not giving in. He knows
how the battle was won, but he still wonders whether he will
ever again look at an ocean swell without charting its course

---

* "Commercial Fishing Safety: Falls Overboard," National Institute
for Occupational Safety and Health, Centers for Disease Control and
Prevention, www.cdc.gov/niosh/topics/fishing/fallsoverboard.html.

and speed and recalling how he both fought and rode similar swells.

Every time the *Anna Mary* goes out to its trawling grounds, it follows the same track up to and past the spot where Johnny went overboard. That's when the memories come. If the *Anna Mary* goes out before dawn, by 6:00 a.m. he may start thinking that by that same hour on July 24, 2013, he had been in the water for three hours, fighting the ocean and his own terror and despair. By three in the afternoon he may hear himself thinking, *How did I endure being in the water all this time?* At moments like that he *sees* it all again, feels himself saturated all over—shoulders, hair, ears, eyes, mouth—and remembers how much work it was. *How did I do it?* he wonders. *How did I endure it?*

One night, three years after his ordeal and rescue, finding himself again alone on watch aboard the *Anna Mary*, Johnny decided to toss an empty bait box over the side to see how long it would take until it was out of sight. It was at the same spot where he went over. The conditions were the same—a calm summer night, the lights of the *Anna Mary* full on, a bit of moonlight as well. Aldridge set up his video camera, turned it on, then flung the corrugated cardboard box out the back of the boat.

It was out of sight at the seventeen-second mark. "That is a *long* time," he says, "to feel your life slip away." It is not hard to remember the fear, as he puts it, of "being the box." He pauses, reliving the fear. "Crazy," he says a moment later.

Aldridge also talks about the experience a lot, which may be another reason he is not particularly plagued by nightmares. People ask him about it all the time. Most days he can nod his head and answer their questions. He can acknowledge what he lived through, and that may keep the nightmares at bay.

He also speaks frequently in formal settings and situations, addressing Coast Guard gatherings, school assemblies, or crowds at community events. And talking, psychologists tell us, can be something of a cure for the malady of posttraumatic stress. No one is exactly certain why that is so. Perhaps it's because in order to put something "out there," you must actively retrieve it from the place within you where it's festering—expose it to the cleansing power of sunlight, so to speak. Perhaps it's because by talking about it, you gain control over the nightmare. Perhaps it's simply that each time you pass the story along, you relinquish a little bit more of it to others— you're no longer the only one carrying the burden. Whatever the reason, Johnny has been telling the story for years.

He was the keynote speaker at the 2014 Pacific Marine Expo, has been interviewed online and in print, has become a spokesman for boat safety, and has filmed a YouTube narrative of his ordeal for the Coast Guard. There's probably little he won't do for the Coast Guard. Within a week of his return home to Montauk Johnny had connected with all the folks at the Montauk Station—lots of family members showing up with him, bringing cookies, expressing their thanks. Those ties persist to this day, even though most station personnel from 2013 are long gone. He has also visited the sector command center in New Haven, the coordinating nerve center for his own rescue. There is a new batch of personnel there as well, but everyone likes to hear from Johnny Aldridge—he is a poster-child for SAR success.

For a while what nearly happened to Johnny Aldridge galvanized the commercial fishing community of Montauk to raise its game where marine safety was concerned. EPIRBS—Emergency Position-Indicating Radio Beacons, personal tracking transmitters that can alert search-and-rescue services to within 150 feet of your location, plus or minus—were much talked about, while life jackets, long a requirement, were at least aired out. Watch alarms enjoyed a vogue. You set an alarm to beep an alert at five- or ten- or fifteen-minute increments, and if the person on watch doesn't respond to the alert, the alarm goes off. But EPIRBS are costly, life jackets are uncomfortable and unwieldy when you're hauling traps, and a lot of fishermen—Anthony is one—don't want to be bothered to set an alarm that's going to beep at them constantly, so bit by bit Montauk's fishermen fell back to the default position of just winging it. What *has* persisted is the memory of what happened to someone everyone knows and likes, and that in itself has made the fishermen, already careful out of necessity, still more watchful. They see him, living proof of what could happen to them, and they remember how vulnerable they are.

That goes for the crew of the *Anna Mary* too. Johnny Aldridge has an EPIRB, but he tends to wear it more in winter than in summer. Anthony does not wear one, not even in winter. "If you go overboard in winter," he says, "you're dead anyway." The watch alarm they bought has been relegated to the electronic-device netherworld. At least both men are mindful about working alone on deck when the rest of the crew is sleeping—simply put, they don't do it. And there has been one noticeable physical change to the boat: the stern is now open only while the crew is hauling traps. The rest of the time it is closed by a newly affixed tailgate.

In personal terms the two men continue in their partnership/friendship that may be as good an example of the marriage of true minds as there is. Linked by a formal business partnership, by the past, and by the passion for fishing they share and don't have to explain to one another, they nevertheless live their separate lives and pursue their different interests. Sosinski remains committed to the full-time care of his father, with whom he still winters on St. John, his "straight-up paradise." The Sosinski daughters—both self-sufficient adults now, one a social worker, the other an aesthetician—and the only Sosinski son-in-law, thus far, tend to gather there at some point in the winter also, and grandfatherhood is expanding the size of those family reunions. When he is in Montauk, Anthony involves himself with LICOP, Long Island Communities of Practice, a not-for-profit organization that runs educational, social, and recreational programs year-round for kids with disabilities and their families. He is particularly committed to working with autistic children and what he calls their "overstressed parents." He has led bowling outings, baton walks, swim lessons, and surfboard lessons for affected kids. No one who knows him is surprised to learn that he is very good at this, and he is certainly passionate about doing it.

Two years after he returned safe and intact from his ordeal, Johnny Aldridge suffered an accident with the pot hauler on the *Anna Mary*, the winching apparatus that raises the traps up from the ocean floor. The upshot was that he managed to lop off the top joint of the middle finger of his right hand. In anger and disgust—and probably in a state of low-grade shock—Aldridge tossed the minuscule body part overboard, thus making it necessary for him to adapt the ways he uses that hand and to relearn numerous actions that once were automatic. He has done this successfully.

But Laurie Zapolski suggests that the shock and anger Johnny expressed over the accident was the delayed playback of what he might have been expected to feel from the ordeal of falling overboard. "He had no time to feel it back then," she guesses, so he more or less let it all out with the loss of part of his finger, which he confronts every day.

Up close those who know him best see some changes in Johnny Aldridge. Mike Skarimbas is certain that "things affect him differently from the way they used to." But he is fundamentally the same man.

He is still the guy who relishes living in Montauk, going for long walks on the beach or in the woods, taking his nephew Jake out on the boat, finding a nearby island, putting out a little seine net, and seeing what Jake hauls in. In the winter he and Laurie are ready to travel in search of new adventures and maybe warmer temperatures when the days grow raw. But for the rest of the year they favor the East End and the ease it affords for the pursuits of ocean-side life—beach time, crabbing, clamming, flatland biking, and the like. Perhaps as a respite from the quiet, Johnny likes to watch the professional drag-racing run by the National Hot Rod Association, both on television and in person at tracks not too far away—Englishtown in New Jersey, Maple Grove in Pennsylvania. He loves to "be around that much horsepower." He has a new hobby too: he has undertaken the restoration of an ancient Corvette, an exacting task for which his meticulous mind is well suited. Aldridge continues to give talks about what happened to him, but mostly, whenever he can, he likes to go fishing.

What happened to Johnny continues to adhere to the lives of both men. Outside of their families and the East End community, it is mostly what they are known for. And for Aldridge it threatens to be what defines him. Those who know him say it's really just the opposite: he defined the event, not the other way around. But the world at large may not see it that way.

One thing the world at large can get a good look at in the story of Johnny Aldridge is the US Coast Guard, an arm of the military that, in truth, not many people know or think much about—certainly not many people who don't live on or near coastline or waterways. Commercial fishermen in general have long held the Coast Guard, which polices certain of their activities, at arm's length: the saying is that the only time the crew of a fishing vessel likes to see the Coast Guard is when the boat or crew is in trouble. Understandable. But when fellow fisherman Johnny Aldridge got into the very worst kind of trouble, his colleagues saw firsthand what the Coast Guard was capable of.

So did a wider public, as the Johnny Aldridge story briefly dominated the news cycle in the nation's biggest media market. Even to those close to the story, what the Coast Guard did was a revelation. Anthony Sosinski marvels that the US government, which everyone complains about and some people he knows consistently rail against, in effect dropped everything, turned on a dime, and in its manifestation as the least-known arm of the military, the US Coast Guard, deployed an astounding array of resources and the most skilled operatives in the search-and-rescue field, as Sosinski puts it, "to find and save one guy!" No one has been heard to protest that the rescue of Johnny Aldridge was an excessive expenditure of taxpayer money. On the contrary: whether or not you know Johnny Aldridge, it was money well spent.*

Yet there is a conundrum at the heart of the John Aldridge SAR that won't quite go away. It's the slight mismatch between the most advanced search-and-rescue capabilities in the world and the unmeasurable and unpredictable will to survive of a human being who is the object of a search.

The analytical capabilities of SAROPS to compute the probable location of a lost object—in this case, John Aldridge—are unquestionably extraordinary. The picture created on

---

* How much was it? The USCG calculates standard hourly rates for inside-government operating costs for assets used in a SAR mission; total inside costs include direct costs, support costs, and general and administrative costs. Adding up just the direct costs for the physical assets deployed by the Coast Guard—one motor lifeboat, one small response boat, one helicopter, one fixed-wing aircraft, and two cutters—yields an hourly cost of $28,662 for the John Aldridge SAR. For an eight-and-a-half-hour search, the total would be in excess of $240,000. That does not, of course, include the costs for such support and administrative resources as personnel, use of the NOAA satellite, and administrative functions from the National Command Center on down, expended to find and rescue Johnny Aldridge.

the SAROPS monitor by a weighted set of particles continually modifies itself, pretty much in real time, adjusting for changes in current, winds, and leeway divergence, which shift constantly on the ocean. It shows search planners, more powerfully than the numbers constantly being input to form the picture could tell them, where the search object is most likely to be and what is happening in that likely location. The system also accounts for the type of "object" being searched— whether a person or something inanimate like a raft—and for the fact that not only is the search object moving but so are the aircraft and vessels searching for the object. SAROPS embraces all that and more, and if and when its target location proves unsuccessful, it folds the failure back into its calculations as it computes a new search location.

But underlying all this very powerful analysis and calculation is the assumption that the search object is drifting—almost certainly true in the case of a raft and profoundly likely in the case of living persons, with or without a flotation device. Typically SAROPS will assign the first search-and-rescue unit to start with the mean drift—to take an average—and it will update and correct from there, continually eliminating search overlap as it moves from average to specific, to more specific, to highly specific. The SAROPS search patterns in the Aldridge SAR did just that. In effect, they started out by just splitting the difference, for at the very beginning of the search all they had to go on was that Johnny was not on the boat, was last seen at nine o'clock the previous night, and was not wearing his flotation device. No one knew when, where, how, or why he had gone overboard nor whether they were looking for a live person or a corpse. As Anthony and the

SAROPS planners were able to zero in on the more likely time and place of Johnny's mishap, the system responded, and the search was adjusted—until SAROPS crashed. But the fact is that the underlying assumption was always that Aldridge would be drifting, that if alive, he would let himself drift or would be powerless to do anything else; if dead, his body would float along the trajectory of drift. In a sense that assumption is the obvious default position, the only one to which the hard data the planners began to receive could add value and bring understanding. Any other default assumption can only lead to guesswork.

Johnny Aldridge, we now know, did not just drift. He sometimes defied and sometimes made use of the drift trajectory that SAROPS was so brilliantly charting. One result was that the early search patterns rolling off the computer program therefore sent USCG assets farther to the west than Johnny's actual location. Johnny knew it, but the Coasties and the civilian volunteer crews with their eyes trained on the ocean for hours on end could not know it.

Make no mistake: Johnny Aldridge was found within the boundaries of the search area SAROPS came up with—he was "in our particles," as one Coastie put it. And as has been noted before in this book, there is no algorithm that can dimension the human will to live, probe the human brain, or divine human intention.

From the moment he filled his boots with air and stopped panicking—"panic is the killer," as Mark Averill has said—John Aldridge was master of his own actions. The strength of his mind is what kept him alive—the ability to put aside the fear and despair that kept rising up in his brain, the ability to deny whatever did not advance survival—and it is what defines him. He used his brain to control his emotions and to analyze, assess, and choose what he would do next. His choice was to make himself as visible as he could. The Coast Guard, with its enormous technological capabilities and array of assets, could not possibly read his mind or discern that choice. What it could do was use the data it gathered, narrow the search, and keep looking. Rescue came when the two sets of mastery, Aldridge's and the Coast Guard's, met.

That's why Sean Davis, the US Coast Guard's operations specialist and the "voice" of the Johnny Aldridge search-and-rescue effort, gets the last word: "We were determined that we would not quit till we found him," Davis has said, "and he kept himself alive long enough for us to do so."

Appendix A

Assets Deployed to Find and Rescue John Aldridge

The SAR case was initiated at 6:22 a.m., EST, the morning of July 24, 2013, when the distress call was received from the fishing vessel *Anna Mary*. The first search asset, Montauk Station's forty-seven-foot motor lifeboat, had launched by 6:54 a.m., and the search by all assets was ended at 3:05 p.m. when the Coast Guard's MH-6002 helicopter reported that Aldridge was aboard the aircraft, alive and well. The eight-and-a-half-hour search covered an area of 660 square miles before Aldridge was spotted by the MH-6002 some 43 miles south of Montauk, New York. The following assets were deployed to participate in the search and successful rescue:

US COAST GUARD ASSETS

From Station New Haven
Central command center of Coast Guard operations for Long Island Sound—known as Sector Long Island Sound—including the south shore of Long Island and along coastal Connecticut. Station is located on the eastern side of New Haven Harbor. Nine other

field subunits, strategically located throughout the Sound, work for this office. This includes approximately five hundred active duty, two hundred reservists, and twelve hundred volunteer CG auxiliary members.

From Station Montauk

CG-47279, forty-seven-foot motor lifeboat (MLB), designed to perform heavy weather rescue in hurricane force winds and twenty-foot breaking seas. This all-aluminum marine innovation withstands impacts of three times the acceleration of gravity and can even survive a complete roll-over, self-righting in less than ten seconds with all machinery remaining fully operational.

Length: 47 feet
Beam: 15 feet
Draft: 4 feet, 6 inches
Max HP: 870 horsepower at 2100 RPM

The forty-seven-foot MLB is primarily designed for fast-response rescue in high seas up to thirty feet, surf up to twenty feet, and heavy weather environments—including winds up to fifty knots. With safety in mind, thirteen water-tight compartments were constructed; the forty-seven-foot MLB can self-right in only thirty seconds. With state-of-the-art electronically controlled engines, fuel-management systems, and an integrated electronics suite, including four coxswain control stations, the forty-seven-foot MLB has become the ideal platform for operations in extreme at-seas weather conditions. As of this writing, 117 forty-seven-foot MLBs are in service throughout the Coast Guard Rescue Station community, serving the public.

CG-25540, twenty-five-foot response boat–Homeland Security (RB-HS), defender class. An aluminum-hulled vessel, equipped with a rigid foam-filled flotation collar.

Length: 25 feet
Beam: 8 feet, 6 inches
Draft: 3 feet, 3 inches
Max HP: 450 horsepower

From Air Station Cape Cod

US Coast Guard Air Station Cape Cod (ASCC), with its four MH-60 Jayhawk-class helicopters and three HC-144A ocean sentry fixed-wing aircraft, is the only Coast Guard Aviation facility in the northeast. As such, ASCC is responsible for the waters from New Jersey to the Canadian border. Centrally located at Joint Base Cape Cod, ASCC maintains the ability to launch a helicopter and/or fixed-wing aircraft within thirty minutes of a call, 365 days a year, twenty-four hours a day, and in nearly all weather conditions.

From here were deployed one MH-60 Jayhawk helicopter and one EADS HC-144 ocean sentry.

The MH-60 Jayhawk is a multimission, twin-engine, medium-range helicopter operated for search-and-rescue, law enforcement, military readiness, and marine environmental protection missions.

Top speed: 207 miles per hour
Range: 807.8 miles
Weight: 14,510 pounds
Wingspan: 54 feet

The EADS HC-144 ocean sentry is a medium-range, twin-engined surveillance aircraft used in search-and-rescue and maritime patrol missions.

Afloat:
Two 87-foot cutters:
USCGC *Sailfish* **(WPB 87356) Sandy Hook, New Jersey**

USCGC *Tiger Shark* **(WPB 87359) Newport, Rhode Island**

VOLUNTEER FLEET: VESSEL, CAPTAIN/OPERATOR

Act One, Charlie Morici
American Pride, Glenn Bickelman
Billy the Kid, Billy Carman and Kelly Lester
The Breakaway, Richard Etzel
Bookie, Robbo Freeman
Brooke C, Peter Spong

Clover, Chuck Etzel Jr.
Cat in the Hat, Dan Stavola
Daramiscotta, Brian Rade and Richie Rade
Hurry Up, Frank Braddick and Donny Briand
New Species, Mike Skarimbas
Lady K, Vinny Damm
Last Mango, Jimmy Buffett
Leatherneck, Al Schaffer
Leona, Vinny Giedratis
Montauk Marine Basin vessel, captained by Danny Christman and Chris Darenberg
Reanda S, Charlie Weimer Jr.
Two Sea Son, Wesley Peterson
Uihleins rental vessel, captained by Jordan Steele and Brad Bowers
Unnamed private vessel, captained by Charlie Etzel Sr.
Unnamed private vessel, captained by *Kimberly* owner Dan Farnham and David Tuma
Unnamed private vessel, captained by Jet Damm
Viking Five Star, Steven Forsberg and Family

"Good Samaritan" aircraft:
Cessna 182 owned and piloted by retired US Army Lieutenant Colonel Walter George Drago, recipient of the Distinguished Flying Cross for Heroism and active with the US Coast Guard Auxiliary; passenger Chuck Weimer.

"The Tale of Johnny Load"

"The Tale of Johnny Load"
©Written by Nancy Atlas ®BMI Music 2016

Little Anthony woke up in the morning
To do dock and gear and get ice.
By nine in the evening he'd worked sixteen hours,
Not counting the four spent at Liar's.
And Johnny came ready, able and steady.
He said, "Man, the first shift's on me.
Go catch a few winks, down in the brink,
And I'll wake you when the fathoms run deep."
By three in the morning alone Johnny's hauling,
The boat set on course dead ahead.
Johnny pulled with his back,
And the handle just snapped,
And that's where this story begins, they said:

Hey Ho, save Johnny Load.
He fell overboard in the night.
Fifteen north of the canyon,

The moon's his companion.
"With only his boots and a knife," they said,
Hey Ho, save Johnny Load.
He's a fisherman lost out at sea,
And he's counting on you and the Montauk Crew
To bring him back to his *Anna Mary*.

There's a scent in the slick and the sharks come on quick,
So you better play dead to survive.
Lock your eyes on the fins, let your body fall limp,
But keep a murderous grip on your knife.
Stay alive till the sun alerts everyone
That you're just a speck in the sea.
And whatever you do, hold onto your boots,
They'll be praying down at St. Therese, they'll say:

Hey Ho, save Johnny Load.
He's a fisherman lost out at sea.
And he's counting on you and the Montauk Crew
To bring him back to his *Anna Mary*.

The ocean's your mother,
Your bitch, and your lover,
And nobody gets to ride free.
It's a roll of the dice
If she'll let you survive.
So bow down, boys, to the queen.

Now Anthony woke, saw that the handle had broke,
And his head and his heart went on fire.
"Johnny!" he screamed. "Brother, where can you be!
Jesus, man, I hope you're alive."
And the fleets soon amassed, crisscrossing in patterns,
The choppers flew further off shore.
And Johnny could hear, the boats were so near,
But nobody saw him at all.

Now the days come to past and the flags at half mast
And the sun, well, it's starting to drown.
Little Anthony says that "it's full steam ahead.
I'm not going in till he's found."
It's the choppers last pass, and he's barely got gas,
But he's going out past his last call.
Then the radio cracks,
There's something to track . . .
"I see a Mark! Mark! Mark!
Anna Mary, we have your man!
He's alive! He's alive!!!"

'Cause the ocean's your mother,
Your bitch, and your lover,
And nobody gets to ride free.
It's a roll of the dice
If she'll let you survive.
So bow down, boys, to the queen.

Hey Ho, they saved Johnny Load.
He fell overboard in the night.
Fifteen north of the canyon,
The moon's his companion,
With only his boots and a knife.
HEY HO, they saved Captain Load.
He was a fisherman lost out at sea
And he counted on you
and the Montauk Crew.
You brought him back to his *Anna Mary*.
You brought him back to his *Anna Mary*.
You brought him back to his *Anna Mary*.

Index